Devotions
for
DIFFICULT
TIMES

Bible Encouragement for Your Life

ED STRAUSS

BARBOUR BOOKS
An Imprint of Barbour Publishing, Inc.

Published by Barbour Books, an imprint of Barbour Publishing, Inc., P.O. Box 719, Uhrichsville, Ohio 44683, www.barbourbooks.com.

Our mission is to publish and distribute inspirational products offering exceptional value and biblical encouragement to the masses.

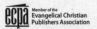 Member of the
Evangelical Christian
Publishers Association

Printed in the United States of America.

Contents

Introduction

Jesus said, "Here on earth you will have many trials and sorrows." It's a promise: You can expect suffering during your lifetime. Jesus went on to say, "But take heart, because I have overcome the world" (John 16:33 NLT). This is good news, but it doesn't necessarily mean the Lord will quickly resolve any difficulties you encounter.

What He offers is not a problem-free life, but the strength to endure your burdens and overcome your tests. Christians today are not spared many of the griefs that assail humanity—including financial pressures, bankruptcies, dysfunctional relationships, marital breakups, accidents, and diseases. This is why God gave us His Word, "that we through the patience and comfort of the Scriptures might have hope" (Romans 15:4 NKJV).

Devotions for Difficult Times draws from these deep wells of encouragement. It was written to breathe life into you when you are forced to walk a very difficult path. It doesn't offer simplistic answers to serious problems, but it does offer hope—real hope—for your darkest hours.

This devotional declares boldly that God will never, ever forsake you, even when your way seems impossible, your circumstances seem unbearable, and you are most tempted to despair. May you find hope in these pages.

Abuse

Close to His Heart

*He tends his flock like a shepherd: he gathers the lambs
in his arms and carries them close to his heart.*
ISAIAH 40:11 NIV

When the disciples tried to keep children away from
Jesus, He said, "Let the little children come to me"
(Mark 10:14 NIV). He then took them in His arms and
blessed them. Gathering the lambs in His arms has
always been Jesus' way.

But if you have suffered abuse or neglect, gone
hungry, or experienced trauma, you may wonder where
the Lord was. And where is He now? The Bible assures
you: "The LORD is close to the brokenhearted" (Psalm
34:18 NIV). God sees your pain. He loves you and cares
deeply for you.

Whatever anyone has done to you, they have done
to Jesus (Matthew 25:34–45), so He empathizes with
your suffering. "In all their suffering he also suffered"
(Isaiah 63:9 NLT). This is one reason Jesus was called
"a man of sorrows, and acquainted with grief" (Isaiah
53:3 KJV).

God not only knows when you experience grief,
but He feels your pain and is there to comfort you if
you will let Him.

Recovering from Abuse

*"O you afflicted one, tossed with tempest,
and not comforted. . . . You shall be far from
oppression, for you shall not fear."*
ISAIAH 54:11, 14 NKJV

In these verses, God speaks to an afflicted person who has suffered from oppressors. Then He describes how she will be rebuilt with precious stones like a beautiful spiritual city (vv. 11–12). The imagery God invokes is strikingly similar to the heavenly Jerusalem in Revelation 21–22, and the similarity is intentional.

Have you suffered abuse in some form? Are you unable to find lasting comfort? Know that God can help you to gain victory over trauma, and He longs for you to experience peace. You can begin to enjoy a foretaste of heaven here and now.

God is able to restore your life and to build you up spiritually so that you will be strong and radiant. Allow His Holy Spirit to enter the darkest corners of your memories, wash away the fear, and cleanse you from guilt, anger, and insecurity.

Recovering from abuse can take years, but God can throw aside the curtains in sudden moments of revelation and splash His sunlight into your soul.

God Sees Your Plight

The Egyptians abused and battered us,
in a cruel and savage slavery.
DEUTERONOMY 26:6 MSG

Women trapped in abusive relationships and children from dysfunctional families can identify with those words, "abused and battered," yet they describe the desperate plight of God's people in Egypt thirty-five hundred years ago.

The next verse says, "We cried out to God. . . . He listened to our voice, he saw our destitution, our trouble, our cruel plight" (Deuteronomy 26:7 MSG). "The Israelites groaned in their slavery and cried out, and their cry for help. . .went up to God" (Exodus 2:23 NIV). God heard them and set them free.

God knows the suffering you have endured, He hears your prayers, and His heart is moved. He will take steps to deliver you from your plight and to comfort you.

He is with you, even in the silence and loneliness, and in your darkest moments when you feel the most damaged and worthless, He looks on you as His own child, of inestimable worth. One day you will meet Him face-to-face and He will wipe all tears from your eyes (Revelation 7:17). In the meantime, He is always with you, comforting you.

Overcoming the Past

*"You make victims of the children and leave them
vulnerable to violence and vice."*
MICAH 2:9 MSG

Frequently, children who are victims of abuse, violence, or neglect grow up insecure and, in later years, look for approval and acceptance in the wrong places. They may seek solace in alcohol or drugs, or search for fulfillment in unhealthy relationships, where they are vulnerable to further violence and vice.

You really have to admire those who had traumatic childhoods and yet are resolving and overcoming their issues to find wholeness and fulfillment. But it is not easy. God offers healing, but it takes a determination to rise above the past, to close the door to anger, and to build a new life in Christ.

"If anyone is in Christ, he is a new creation; old things have passed away; behold, all things have become new" (2 Corinthians 5:17 NKJV). God does a major work in people's heart at salvation, but complete transformation takes a lifetime. "We. . .beholding as in a mirror the glory of the Lord, are being transformed into the same image" (2 Corinthians 3:18 NKJV).

It takes time, but we are being transformed.

Accidents

Occupational Hazards

When you chop wood,
there is danger with each stroke of your ax.
ECCLESIASTES 10:9 NLT

When you are injured on the job, you are filled with conflicting thoughts. On the one hand, you know that all occupations have hazards. Soldiers, policemen, and firemen are aware that their jobs are dangerous, but even desk jobs have liabilities.

Still, you may wonder, *Why didn't God protect me?* After all, the Bible promises, "If you. . .make the Most High your dwelling, no harm will overtake you, no disaster will come near your tent. For he will command his angels concerning you to guard you in all your ways" (Psalm 91:9–11 NIV).

Staying close to God definitely guards you from a great deal of misfortune, but the fact is, it won't guarantee you a completely trouble-free existence. The Bible states, "People are born for trouble as readily as sparks fly up from a fire" (Job 5:7 NLT). That's the way life is. We all get sick. We all feel pain. We all have accidents.

But the good news is: "There is wonderful joy ahead, even though you must endure many trials for a little while" (1 Peter 1:6 NLT).

Unexpected Injuries

Ahaziah had fallen through the lattice of his upper
room in Samaria and injured himself.
2 KINGS 1:2 NIV

In Bible times, people covered their window openings with thin slats of wood called latticework. One day King Ahaziah was in an upper palace room and leaned heavily against the latticework, causing it to break. He plunged to the courtyard below and was seriously injured (2 Kings 1:2). Because he looked to the false god Baal-Zebub for healing, he died (vv. 16–17).

You may trust in God, but that is not a guarantee that you will never have an accident. The difference is that God constantly works on behalf of His children to bring great good out of tragedies. "All things work together for good to those who love God" (Romans 8:28 NKJV), even accidents.

When you suffer unexpected misfortune, God can see to it that you also experience unexpected good as a result—benefits such as spiritual depth, compassion, and patience.

You might rather do without spiritual benefits and simply enjoy a trouble-free, easy life, but God is seeking to transform you into a better person, and to do so, He often has to bring you through troubled times.

Unexplained Misfortune

No one can predict misfortune. . . . So men and women
are caught by accidents evil and sudden.
ECCLESIASTES 9:12 MSG

Many Christians believe that nothing happens randomly. They insist that God is in control of events down to the very tiniest details. And since He is able to protect them from all accidents and misfortune, when accidents happen God must have good reasons for allowing them, even if these reasons aren't apparent.

This is true, but to focus on that is to miss the big picture. God is definitely able to micromanage events in believers' lives to bring about His purposes, but it is important to realize that He is focused on the larger issues. The psalmist said of God, "Your thoughts are very deep" (Psalm 92:5 NKJV).

Some people demand, "Why, God?" They insist that God explain His actions. They desire an itemized justification for every injury He allowed. Meanwhile, God's concern is the overall condition of their heart. He is watching whether they will trust Him no matter what.

The fact is, most times in this life you won't understand why God has allowed an accident. So focus on what's most important—loving Him and remaining true to Him through it all.

Guarded from Evil

*They will lift you up in their hands, so that you will
not strike your foot against a stone.*
PSALM 91:12 NIV

You may be confused when reading the promises of
Psalm 91. Verse 11 (NIV) says that God's angels will
"guard you in all your ways." The very next verse promises that they won't even allow you to stub your toe
against a stone. However, you know from experience
that you and most other believers do suffer injury from
time to time, sometimes even serious injuries.

Yet the psalm promises, "No harm will overtake
you" (v. 10 NIV). It sounds like you should expect to
experience a totally blessed, trouble-free life. So what
gives?

The answer is that this is the ideal state, promised when you passionately love God and know Him
(v. 14). The opening verse states that these promises are
for "whoever dwells in the shelter of the Most High"
(v. 1). You must *constantly* dwell close to God's heart,
sheltered by His presence.

Most Christians don't abide that close to God. So
although He still protects you, often in direct correla-
tion to how close you are to Him, you will occasionally
suffer accidents.

Accidents and Judgment

"What about the eighteen people who died when the tower in Siloam fell on them? Were they the worst sinners in Jerusalem?"
LUKE 13:4 NLT

Many Jews believed there were no such things as "accidents." Whenever something bad happened to someone, it was considered God's judgment on sin.

But at a certain level, this rationale breaks down. After all, carpenters use sharp tools to cut wood and end up with nicks and cuts fairly frequently (Ecclesiastes 10:9). So only the *biggest* accidents were considered judgments—but even so, this isn't a cause-and-effect rule that applies in every case.

Proverbs 26:27 (NKJV) says, "He who rolls a stone will have it roll back on him," so when eighteen people were killed by collapsing stones, many Jews were absolutely convinced that those men had been the worst sinners in the city. But Jesus disputed this.

He said that those men had been no worse than the people standing around pointing their fingers. They all were sinners, so it could have happened to any of them (Luke 13:5). Now, God sometimes does judge sin by allowing accidents, but only He knows each situation, so let's stop judging others.

Addiction

Caught in a Vicious Cycle

A man of great wrath shall suffer punishment:
for if thou deliver him, yet thou must do it again.
PROVERBS 19:19 KJV

When you have an addiction, you find yourself compulsively indulging in harmful behavior, even though you know it is destructive. This is true for those prone to anger, but it is also true if your addiction is gambling, overeating, pornography, spending, or alcohol.

Someone may mercifully step in and deliver you from the mess you make of your life, and cushion the consequences of your actions, but does that really help? They will just have to do it again next week.

If you have an addiction, Paul's words describe your dilemma: "I obviously need help! . . . I can will it, but I can't do it. I decide to do good, but I don't really do it; I decide not to do bad, but then I do it anyway. . . . Is there no one who can do anything for me? . . . The answer, thank God, is that Jesus Christ can and does" (Romans 7:18–19, 24–25 MSG).

When you finally come to the end of yourself, you are ready for God's solution.

Lust and Pornography

"I have made a covenant with my eyes;
why then should I look upon a young woman?"
JOB 31:1 NKJV

Many men are addicted to pornography. It starts "harm-lessly." They allow their eyes to linger a few seconds on attractive women—in person or in the media—while entertaining fleeting thoughts of sexual pleasure. If they make little effort to resist such thoughts, they become more frequent. Eventually, they begin visiting explicit websites.

They can become addicted to the rushes of excite-ment, which are, however, followed by guilt and a weakened prayer life. Paul promises, "No temptation has overtaken you except such as is common to man; but God. . .will also make the way of escape, that you may be able to bear it" (1 Corinthians 10:13 NKJV).

Four thousand years ago, Job said, "I have made a covenant with my eyes" (Job 31:1 NKJV). Job knew he had to nip lust in the bud. So he made a firm decision not to allow his eyes to linger on a young woman, not to indulge in even a fleeting lust.

He stopped lust cold—and it kept him from a great deal of trouble.

Stuck in the Mud

"A sow that is washed returns to her
wallowing in the mud."
2 PETER 2:22 NIV

One of the most frustrating things about an addiction is that even though you recognize that it is wreaking havoc in your life, and you make a decision to stop it, it often has such a powerful grip that before you know it, you are at it again.

Although it isn't flattering to envision yourself like a pig rolling in the mud, it may be helpful to look at your addiction in light of this statement. The point of the word picture is that simply attempting to clean up your act on the outside isn't enough. Until you have a change in your basic nature, you will continually return to your addiction after attempts to stop.

That is why you need the life-changing power of the Holy Spirit to take hold of your mind and spirit and bring about lasting change. This usually takes time, and it will certainly take repeated, desperate prayers. You have to really want change, doggedly pursue God, and not give up until He answers your prayers.

Fortunately, God continually gives you another chance, even after you mess up again.

Addicted to Pleasure

You're addicted to thrills? What an empty life!
The pursuit of pleasure is never satisfied.
PROVERBS 21:17 MSG

Addictions come in many forms. Some people are addicted to prescription drugs. Many people are addicted to the love hormones, dopamine and norepinephrine, and constantly seek thrills from illicit sexual encounters. They "live for lustful pleasure" (Ephesians 4:19 NLT). Some people's brains release dopamine when they are engaged in extreme sports. They receive a pleasurable reward from high-risk activities and so repeatedly come back for more.

But whether the thrills people pursue are illegal, immoral, or simply insanely dangerous, the Bible says that the constant pursuit of pleasure is never satisfied. A life lived only for selfish pleasure and fulfillment is empty, and it often becomes expensive very quickly. "Those who love pleasure become poor; those who love wine and luxury will never be rich" (Proverbs 21:17 NLT).

People are addicted to things and substances for the rewards they give them. If you want to break free from such addictions and truly enjoy life, you have to find fulfillment in God. "In Your presence is fullness of joy; at Your right hand are pleasures forevermore" (Psalm 16:11 NKJV).

Adultery

Adultery Is Destructive

Adultery is a brainless act,
soul-destroying, self-destructive.
PROVERBS 6:32 MSG

Adultery truly is a mindless act. It is not that adulterers have no brain; the problem is that they are not listening to it. Against their better judgment, in the face of all they know to be true and right, they ignore their rational minds and allow their bodies to be swept along in a tidal wave of lust. Perhaps this tragedy has happened to you—or to your spouse.

God designed the love hormones, dopamine and norepinephrine, to create intense feelings of excitement and romantic passion. He intended a husband and wife to enjoy the pleasures of sex to the full. But He doesn't sanction sex outside of marriage. His Word tells us, "Marriage is honorable among all, and the bed undefiled; but fornicators and adulterers God will judge" (Hebrews 13:4 NKJV).

Now, God will one day judge adulterers, but in the meantime, "a man who commits adultery. . .destroys himself" (Proverbs 6:32 NIV). He destroys integrity, love, trust, his marriage, and sometimes his entire life. If you have gone astray in this way, turn to God and He will have mercy on you.

Adultery in the Heart

*"Anyone who looks at a woman lustfully has already
committed adultery with her in his heart."*
MATTHEW 5:28 NIV

Some of Jesus' listeners were astonished when He
informed them that a man who looks at a woman with
sexual lust and fantasizes about having sex with her has
already committed adultery with her in his heart. But
that is precisely what he is doing. Jesus didn't say the
man had literally committed adultery. He said the man
had done it "in his heart."

The Lord also wasn't talking about a passing
thought—something most people experience—which
they immediately resist. Some people have been needlessly condemned over this. Jesus was talking about
focusing on someone with intense desire.

Most people, when they fantasize about having an
adulterous affair, purposefully fill their thoughts with
lurid mental images. This is what Moses was warning against when he wrote, "You shall not covet your
neighbor's wife" (Deuteronomy 5:21 NIV). To "covet"
means to earnestly, persistently desire, to set one's heart
on something.

Eventually this leads to thoughts of how to actually *have* that person, not merely imagine it. That is
why it is vital not to even start down that path.

Obsessed with Adultery

They're obsessed with adultery, compulsive in sin,
seducing every vulnerable soul they come upon.
2 PETER 2:14 MSG

Many men and women are addicted to adultery. It gives them a rush. They are constantly on the lookout for dissatisfied married people who can be flattered and enticed to indulge in an illicit affair. Many men "creep into households and make captives of gullible women loaded down with sins, led away by various lusts" (2 Timothy 3:6 NKJV).

Of course, some women are the initiators. Like Potiphar's wife, they are continuously looking for new bed partners (Genesis 39:7–12). The Bible warns, "Don't. . .be taken in by her bedroom eyes" (Proverbs 6:25 MSG). And though "the lips of the adulterous woman drip honey" (Proverbs 5:3 NIV), they lead to death.

God knows that even though you are married, you will still find other members of the opposite sex attractive, and at times your hormones will fill you with powerful waves of desire. But don't give in to them, or the day will come when you deeply regret it. Once you have betrayed your husband or wife, it can take a long time and many prayers and tears to rebuild his or her trust.

Commonsense Commandment

You must not commit adultery.
EXODUS 20:14 NLT

Five short words, but they serve to safeguard you from a very destructive sin. God knew that most people would—at some point or another—be tempted to commit adultery, so He put up a billboard commanding you not to do it.

Remember, "no temptation has overtaken you except what is *common* to mankind" (1 Corinthians 10:13 NIV, emphasis added).

Sexual attraction is a powerful force, and God designed it to help bond husbands and wives together. But even believers, if they are not careful, can be overcome by the siren call of extramarital sex. That is why you must internalize God's command and take steps to keep yourself safe.

You can't keep from noticing that someone is sexually attractive—especially if they have gone to pains to make themselves look that way—but you can keep your eyes from sneaking back for a second and third glance.

If you find your imagination constantly excited by someone else's husband or wife, persistently resist such thoughts. Take definite steps to make sure that you don't ever end up alone with that person. Do these things and God will keep you from falling.

Heating Up Ovens

"They are all adulterers. Like an oven heated by a baker. . . . They are all hot, like an oven."
HOSEA 7:4, 7 NKJV

Feelings of sexual desire can be very powerful. Such passion is entirely appropriate with your husband or wife, but inappropriate outside marriage.

Hosea compared the adulterers of Israel to "an oven heated by a baker," where the baker added fuel to the barely burning coals in the oven. Hosea 7:4 (NKJV) adds, "He ceases stirring the fire after kneading the dough." But up until that time the baker had worked to *stir up* a blazing fire.

Just so, people who commit adultery usually feed the flames of desire with sexual images. Adultery is often a deliberate, premeditated act. One good way to avoid this is to get rid of any fuel so you can't feed the fire. This means ridding your home of pornography and refusing to view it on the Internet. Doing these things will greatly reduce the problem.

In addition, remember the Bible's advice: "It is better to marry than to burn with passion" (1 Corinthians 7:9 NKJV). And if you are already married, be satisfied with that (Proverbs 5:18–20).

Alcohol Abuse

Overcoming Alcoholism

Who has needless bruises? Who has bloodshot eyes?
Those who linger over wine.
PROVERBS 23:29–30 NIV

If you have a problem with alcohol, you don't need to be told that it is wrong. You already know that. You know that it is wasting your hard-earned cash, that it is wrecking your marriage, and that it leaves you filled with remorse and despair. And then there are those bruises you can't explain from bumping into things. The question is, what are you going to do about it?

Until you are desperate enough to surrender your life to God, there is not a whole lot you can do. You have already tried to stop yourself but have repeatedly fallen off the wagon.

Here is where the biblical principles behind Alcoholics Anonymous can help: You must honestly admit your sins, confess your faults to someone else, and trust God for the power to change. There is more to it, but these things are an excellent start.

As a Christian, you know that the Higher Power is Jesus, the Son of God. He said, "Apart from me you can do nothing" (John 15:5 NIV). And Paul wrote, "I can do everything through Christ, who gives me strength" (Philippians 4:13 NLT).

Downsides of Alcohol

Wine produces mockers; alcohol leads to brawls.
Those led astray by drink cannot be wise.
PROVERBS 20:1 NLT

Alcohol removes inhibitions and sets people's base natures loose. A person under the influence of drink is often loud and confrontational. Some people become happy and make jokes or boast; others become angry and mock or argue. The latter often leads to drunken fights.

"Those led astray by drink cannot be wise." Have you ever seen an inebriated man giving someone advice? Though he may think he is sharing words of profound wisdom, to the sober listener it is utter foolishness.

The only time you can be truly wise is when you are sober. That is when it pays to take a long, hard look at the benefits and downsides of drinking. Alcohol does offer a temporary escape from trouble. This is why many people turn to it to unwind and forget, or to have a "good time." Unfortunately, it also causes many problems, problems that are not temporary.

If you struggle with alcohol, it is wise to make yourself accountable to others who understand your struggle. Listen to their advice and then act on it day by day.

Boasting about Drinking

*What sorrow for those who are heroes at drinking
wine and boast about all the alcohol they can hold.*
ISAIAH 5:22 NLT

Sometimes what you thought was a strength, something to be proud of, was actually a weakness. The fact that you once boasted about your drinking was a sure sign that you had set yourself up for grief. If you now have sobriety, you can look back and shake your head in disbelief at such a mind-set.

If you are still struggling to gain mastery over the bottle, you may already be aware that boasting about how much liquor you can hold is stupid. But knowing that isn't enough. You can still be fooled by thinking, *But one drink can't hurt, since, after all, it takes a lot for me to get drunk.* But one glass leads to many more.

If you have any pride left at all about drinking, or if you are still amused by your antics when intoxicated, you are not ready to abandon alcohol and put your life back together. As cliché as this sounds, you actually have to hit rock bottom before you are ready for God's solution.

Getting Flaming Drunk

What sorrow for those who. . . spend long evenings drinking wine to make themselves flaming drunk.
ISAIAH 5:11 NLT

Those who have a full-blown case of alcoholism have little control over their addiction. However, not all people have an advanced case of this addiction, particularly at the beginning. Often, when they are first giving in to drink, they have a choice in the matter.

That is why the Bible warns you not to binge-drink just to experience what it is like to be completely drunk. Not only are you starting down a very slippery slope that could become a lifelong habit of destruction, but think of the damage you can cause in just one night!

The young are especially tempted to prove how much alcohol they can hold or just how much of a spectacle they are willing to make of themselves. Many see out-of-control drunkenness as a rite of passage or a way to earn respect or acceptance. What sorrow they earn instead!

Why wait until things get so bad that alcohol has become your master and you must fight a protracted battle to take back your life? It is better to stop before you even start.

Anger

Controlling Your Temper

Do not hasten in your spirit to be angry,
for anger rests in the bosom of fools.
ECCLESIASTES 7:9 NKJV

The New International Version says it this way: "Do not be quickly provoked in your spirit." In other words, exercise self-control and don't allow yourself to be easily provoked. Whether you believe that you can do it or not, God expects you to be able to control your temper.

James writes, "Let every man be. . .slow to wrath" (James 1:19 NKJV), and you might have to bite down on your tongue to avoid giving in to it.

The Bible also says, "A fool's wrath is known at once. . . . A fool rages. . . . A quick-tempered man acts foolishly" (Proverbs 12:16; 14:16, 17 NKJV). Remind yourself: If you continue to lose your temper easily, you are behaving like a fool—and the Bible gives clear warnings about fools: "The mouth of the foolish is near destruction. . . . A fool lays open his folly. . . . The foolishness of a man twists his way. . . . A fool vents all his feelings" (Proverbs 10:14; 13:16; 19:3; 29:11 NKJV). Exercising self-control is well worth it.

Be Slow to Anger

*Let every man be swift to hear,
slow to speak, slow to wrath.*
JAMES 1:19 KJV

Many people are easygoing. They don't rile easily. Other people have a short fuse and struggle with anger issues most of their lives. They know they should simply let things go, but at the slightest provocation, their temper flares up. Is there no solution?

There may not be an easy solution, but there is a solution. James tells us, "Let every man be. . .slow to wrath" (James 1:19 KJV). He says "*every* man." This tells us that with God's help, we all can gain control of our tempers. No exceptions.

However, we often first need to renounce our pride. Some people actually boast, "Whoa! You should see me when I get mad!" The Bible addresses pride-motivated statements, saying, "All such boasting is evil" (James 4:16 NKJV).

Second, they must cry out to God for help. Third, they need to make a constant effort to have patience. If they give others the benefit of the doubt and don't jump to conclusions, they can defuse many arguments and provocations before they begin.

Hot Tempers and Conflict

An angry person stirs up conflict,
and a hot-tempered person commits many sins.
PROVERBS 29:22 NIV

Whether you are an angry person or are close to an angry person, you know how easily someone with a temper can be set off. At the slightest provocation, voices are raised, accusations are made, and the fight is on. Lighting an angry person's fuse is easy, and once lit, the person explodes.

Pride and a brooding sense of injustice are often at the root. Angry people are quick to imagine that someone has insulted them and to take offense. They constantly stir up fights and in the process, commit many sins.

Try this: *Pray* for those who anger you, commit them into God's hands, ask Him to bless them richly, and pray that He will give you love, empathy, and understanding for them. "The LORD turned the captivity of Job, when he prayed for his friends" (Job 42:10 KJV).

When you earnestly pray for others' good, you more easily forgive and overlook their faults. And if you are overlooking their faults, you won't be prone to be angry with them.

Quick-Tempered Folly

Whoever is patient has great understanding,
but one who is quick-tempered displays folly.
PROVERBS 14:29 NIV

If you are plagued by a quick temper, it might seem frustrating to hear that the solution is to have lots of patience—as if there was a choice in the matter! Your anger might appear to be like a tidal wave that rises up in an instant without warning, at the slightest provocation. It might seem as if you have no control over it.

The truth is, however, that you can eventually master it if you are determined to do so. It will take time and concentrated effort, and it may even take attending a few anger management courses. But the more you understand why you react the way you do and recognize your trigger points, the more control you will have.

Another strategy for reining in your temper is to make a concerted effort to understand others as well. If you begin to understand what motivates them, you are less likely to take offense. And if you determine to be patient with people and to love them with God's love, you can actually begin to govern your anger.

Controlling Your Temper

Sensible people control their temper;
they earn respect by overlooking wrongs.
PROVERBS 19:11 NLT

Even smart people can have a quick temper. However, they recognize that their anger is a problem, so they take steps to control it. They don't want to hurt others or make a bad situation worse.

If you have anger issues, there are things you can do. First, the Bible says to overlook wrongs. Solomon said, "Do not pay attention to every word people say," but remind yourself that you, too, say things you shouldn't (Ecclesiastes 7:21–22 NIV). If you can, let it pass.

Second, make up your mind ahead of time that when provoked, you won't respond with an angry outburst.

Third, don't answer quickly, but take time to pray and think through a calm response.

Fourth, when you express yourself, avoid making blanket accusations such as, "You always. . ." Instead, explain how the offender's actions or words make you feel.

Fifth, instead of focusing on what made you angry, suggest solutions to the problem.

Sixth, when really angry, take some time out to exercise.

Seventh, pray and meditate on peaceful subjects before reengaging with the person who offended you.

Anxiety

Avoiding Anxiety

So what do people get. . .for all their hard work and
anxiety?. . .At night their minds cannot rest.
ECCLESIASTES 2:22–23 NLT

A habit of worry leads to an anxious mind. Anxiety is a decision not to trust God, but to instead scramble around trying to solve your own problems. You may find yourself slipping so naturally into a worried attitude that it doesn't even seem like a conscious decision. But it is.

What starts off as a small worry quickly grows into a frenzied effort to work things out. But it is all a waste of time.

The first step to overcoming anxiety is to realize that worrying is a surefire way to sabotage success. Being anxious all day is very tiring, yet it robs you of sleep at night. And knowing that you won't be able to do your best if you are sleep deprived gives you something else to worry about.

The best way to fight anxiety is to continually look to the Lord, constantly quote Bible promises to yourself, and refuse to give an inch to worry. It will be hard at first, but don't worry: It gets easier as time goes on.

Wearing Yourself Out

*It is useless for you to work so hard from early morning
until late at night, anxiously working for food to eat;
for God gives rest to his loved ones.*
PSALM 127:2 NLT

Many people think that worry is a trifling thing, something that frays the outer edges of their minds but
really isn't a problem. But anxiety can suck the very
life out of you. If you fear that setbacks are inevitable
and constantly fret that your finances aren't sufficient,
you will work harder to compensate for the lack. And
if you work when you should be resting, you will wear
yourself out.

The thing is, there may not even be a lack on your
horizon. You just worry that there will be. So you give
yourself stomach ulcers and overwork for nothing.
Now, it is prudent to make sure that you have sufficient
finances, but anxiety is beyond prudent. It's a failure to
believe that God cares for you.

David wrote, "In the multitude of my anxieties
within me, Your comforts delight my soul" (Psalm
94:19 NKJV). David did what he could, but after that
he trusted the Lord and allowed God to comfort him.

Don't Be Anxious

Do not be anxious about anything, but in every situation. . .present your requests to God.
PHILIPPIANS 4:6 NIV

Say you are out shopping and you suddenly realize you have lost your keys or your iPhone. You are hit with panic, and as time crawls on, you get a sinking feeling of how bad this situation is. The normal tendency is to let wave after wave of anxiety roll over you.

But the Bible says, "Do not be anxious about *anything*, but in *every* situation. . .present your requests to God" (Philippians 4:6 NIV, emphasis added). No exceptions. So that is what you should do: Ask God to do a miracle and help you locate it or to have some honest person find it and turn it in.

It doesn't have to be an emergency either. It could simply be a situation that is bad and slowly getting worse, and over which you have little control. Rather than letting it suck the life out of you, you need to be able to turn it over to God.

You aren't guaranteed that God will reunite you with your missing items, but He can at least limit the damage that their loss may cause.

Arguments

Pride and Arguing

By pride comes nothing but strife.
PROVERBS 13:10 NKJV

You may like to think that you are reasonable and that when you disagree with someone, you base your arguments only on facts. But most people are motivated by a number of factors—pride being chief among them.

Try this: Watch others argue and listen to their reasoning and logic. But also observe their facial expressions and body language, and pay attention to the tone of their voices. Do voices become raised and faces become angry and flushed when debating? This is proof that strong emotions are involved. Do they resort to mockery to negate sound reasoning? Do they use humor, sarcasm, or zingers to try to score major points?

Let's face it: Many arguments are caused by nothing but pride. Someone feels threatened and so refuses to acknowledge that the other person is right at all. Or she has been offended and so she bristles up and quarrels. Or he feels mistreated and so he argues out of a sense of injustice—barely even listening to what the other person is saying.

We all have been guilty of these things, so let's walk in a spirit of humility and disagree politely.

Senseless Quarrels

Don't have anything to do with foolish and stupid
arguments, because you know they produce quarrels.
2 TIMOTHY 2:23 NIV

If you happen to walk by two neighbors arguing, and one of them is making ridiculous or irrational claims, you may be tempted to stop and try to set that person straight. Don't. It's very often not worth the trouble.

"Interfering in someone else's argument is as foolish as yanking a dog's ears" (Proverbs 26:17 NLT). What happens when you do that? The dog bites you, of course. For the same reason, Jesus said, "Don't throw your pearls to pigs! They will trample the pearls, then turn and attack you" (Matthew 7:6 NLT).

When people are making pigheaded arguments, they are not open to reason. And many people argue from an emotional basis, which is why they are not convinced by even the most rational explanations.

Don't even answer those seeking to drag you into a quarrel. If they are looking for a fight, there is no way you can win. You will just end up raving like them. "Don't answer the foolish arguments of fools, or you will become as foolish as they are" (Proverbs 26:4 NLT).

Avoid Argumentative People

Stay away from mindless, pointless quarreling.
TITUS 3:9 MSG

There is no way to have a rational discussion with a person who loves to argue. Any disagreement quickly descends into pointless quarreling. They either end up yelling at you or mocking you. "If a wise man contends with a foolish man, whether the fool rages or laughs, there is no peace" (Proverbs 29:9 NKJV).

Do your best to avoid argumentative people. If you can't avoid them, resolutely refuse to be drawn into quarrels with them. It is simply not worth the trouble. And if it means letting them think they got the better of you, let them think that.

This doesn't mean you can't have any relationship with such people. You may have to maintain a rapport with them if they are family members or workmates.

Paul instructed church leaders, "Warn a quarrel-some person once or twice, but then be done with him" (Titus 3:10 MSG). When it becomes obvious that someone is fully set in their ways, you need to have the wisdom to refrain from trying to convince them or change them. Instead, pray for them.

Avoiding Quarrels

Starting a quarrel is like breaching a dam;
so drop the matter before a dispute breaks out.
PROVERBS 17:14 NIV

They didn't have huge hydroelectric dams in Bible days. The dams that existed were usually pond-sized irrigation reservoirs, and the water was held back by walls of hard-packed dirt. One farmer with a pickax could easily breach it. And once the water started to rush out and sweep away more and more of the restraining wall, there was no way to stop it.

Sometimes when you tell a friend you are going to confront somebody, they ask, "Is this the hill you want to die on?" In other words, given its potential for causing unwanted trouble and repercussions, is the confrontation really worth engaging in?

Some issues are well worth disputing, make no mistake about it. But disputing out of pride or to put somebody "in his place," simply isn't worth it. And the problem is, once you start the process, you have stirred up the other person, and the war is on.

How do you know when to contend and when to drop a matter? "A wise man's heart discerns both time and judgment" (Ecclesiastes 8:5 NKJV).

Keep Your Cool

*A servant of the Lord must not quarrel but must be kind
to everyone. . .and be patient with difficult people.*
2 TIMOTHY 2:24 NLT

You may think, *"Be kind to everyone"? Sure, I can manage
that.* But you stop short at the next part: "Be patient
with difficult people." You think, *I don't take grief from
anybody. If someone is ornery, I'll tell them off.* So much
for being kind to *everyone.*

When scripture says you "must not quarrel," it
means exactly that. You must not quarrel even with
cantankerous individuals. And how do you avoid it?
By being kind to everyone.

There is a difference between quarrels and disagreements. Sometimes we have no choice but to dispute with someone, whether the person is ornery or
not. But the main reason we are advised not to quarrel
with difficult persons is that we won't get anywhere by
doing so. We will just waste our time.

Some people love a good argument. For them, it is
important to win a debate, but it is more important to
get the satisfaction of yelling at the other person and
putting that person in his or her place. But that is not
God's way of doing things.

Bankruptcy

When Everything Is Gone

*"My husband is dead, and. . .now his creditor
is coming to take my two boys as his slaves."*
2 KINGS 4:1 NIV

Over a hundred prophets followed Elisha around to learn from him. One of them had a wife and two young boys. They had a small mud-brick house but little else. The prophet apparently became sick and unable to work, so he was forced to borrow money to buy food.

He probably hoped to recover and get back to work, but instead he grew steadily worse and died. The creditor demanded repayment, but since the widow had absolutely nothing, he came to enslave her two sons and work them to pay the debt. But Elisha prayed, and God did a miracle to provide the money she needed.

Bankruptcy wasn't really an option in Old Testament times. People had to pay one way or another. We today can be thankful. Even though bankruptcy is a difficult and humiliating ordeal, and recovery can take years, things aren't as harsh as they were in Elisha's day.

If you have had to declare bankruptcy, thank God for seeing you through it.

Riches to Rags

"The Almighty has made life very bitter for me.
I went away full, but the LORD has
brought me home empty."
RUTH 1:20–21 NLT

During a long drought in Israel, Naomi and her husband, Elimelech, became so desperate that they sold their land to have money for food. When the money ran out, they had to move to Moab in search of employment.

Today both societies and individuals experience financial droughts. You may have gone through a prolonged period of unemployment that drained your savings and forced you to declare bankruptcy.

When this happened, you may have wondered why God decided to make your life bitter. Usually, however, when people go bankrupt, it is not God's doing. Often they are reaping the results of their own financial mismanagement. However, sometimes an entire society goes through a recession. Then many innocent people suffer.

Don't become bitter against God. Trust that He will see you through the crisis. In the meantime, practice what Paul wrote: "I have learned how to be content with whatever I have. I know how to live on almost nothing or with everything" (Philippians 4:11–12 NLT).

Experiencing Financial Ruin

Let the creditor seize all that he has,
and let strangers plunder his labor.
PSALM 109:11 NKJV

Bankruptcy in Bible times was an even more traumatic experience than it is today. When a wicked man was accusing him falsely and fighting against him without just cause, David prayed, "Let the creditor seize all that he has."

This was one of the most devastating things David could have wished on an enemy. A creditor would literally seize *all* that a person had—going so far as to press him and his family into slavery to work off their debt. At least today, if you are forced into bankruptcy, the trustees are supposed to see to it that you are left with enough to live on.

In today's troubled economy, it is not only the wicked and the reckless who experience bankruptcy. Yes, often people end up there due to overspending or financial decisions that, in hindsight, weren't the wisest—but sometimes the innocent are driven into financial ruin by circumstances beyond their control.

God is able to rescue you from the deepest pit you find yourself in and establish your feet on solid ground again.

Hope after Bankruptcy

*I will restore to you the years
that the locust hath eaten.*
JOEL 2:25 KJV

Locusts are a type of winged grasshopper that live, among other places, in the deserts of North Africa. Under certain conditions, they begin to breed abundantly and to migrate. At times they descended on Israel in swarms of eighty billion strong.

They caused unimaginable damage, devouring grain crops and vineyards, and even stripping the leaves off trees. Everyone suffered loss and saw the hard work of years wiped out. God said that He sent locusts as punishment but promised that if His people repented, "I will forgive their sin and will heal their land" (2 Chronicles 7:13–14 NIV).

There is hope of similar healing after bankruptcy. God can likewise restore to you the many years' worth of loss that such an event has wiped out. It will take time, but bankruptcy, hard as it may be, can teach you valuable lessons and a sense of priorities that will serve you well in the future.

If you are going through a bankruptcy or recovering from one, take hope. God is in the business of helping people get back on their feet after heavy losses.

Betrayal

When Friends Betray You

*My best friend, the one I trusted completely,
the one who shared my food, has turned against me.*
PSALM 41:9 NLT

Betrayal hurts, especially when the person who betrayed you was a close friend, someone you shared your most intimate thoughts with. You trusted him. Then you learned that he went about as a gossip, either carelessly or maliciously telling your deepest secrets.

We all have experienced betrayal in one form or another. Perhaps you have betrayed someone. Even if you didn't intentionally cross her, she feels that you did, or that you went back on your word, let her down, or told others things she had confided to you.

It is difficult to make amends if the one you betrayed no longer wishes to speak to you and refuses to trust you again. Since you know how that feels, make sure never to put someone else through the wringer for a similar blunder.

Discern between a malicious betrayal (by someone you must avoid confiding in again) and a friend who made an honest mistake (but who deserves another chance, and whom you can still trust). Forgive everyone, but use wisdom in restoring people to your confidence.

Untrustworthy Gossips

A gadabout gossip can't be trusted with a secret.
PROVERBS 11:13 MSG

Sometimes you let down your guard and tell another person confidential things you probably shouldn't. He is your friend. You trust him. What could go wrong? But misunderstandings happen, and when they do, friends get offended. And then a friend, who now has a grudge against you, is in possession of information that could cause you embarrassment or damage.

Or maybe there was no misunderstanding. Maybe a friend simply wasn't trustworthy to begin with, because she just couldn't resist the temptation to share some juicy gossip.

Sometimes you are blindsided by betrayal. But often you set yourself up for pain by trusting someone against your better judgment. This is why David wrote, "I will hold my tongue when the ungodly are around me" (Psalm 39:1 NLT). And at times you need to refrain from telling *anyone*. "Don't trust your neighbor, don't confide in your friend" (Micah 7:5 MSG).

Of course, you need to be able to share your heart with friends, and fortunately there *are* good, trustworthy people. Know who can be trusted and stick to confiding in them.

A Legacy of Abuse

Those who betray their own friends
leave a legacy of abuse to their children.
JOB 17:5 MSG

Some people are users. They feel that other people exist for their benefit, perhaps to borrow money from (with no intention of repaying) or to use for momentary sexual gratification, and then to toss aside. They befriend people intending to use them and betray their trust.

If you have suffered at the hands of such people, learn to recognize them and to avoid being taken in. Learn to say no to their sob stories, and refuse to let them use you again.

"They are like shameless shepherds who care only for themselves. They are like clouds blowing over the land without giving any rain. . . . They are like wild waves of the sea, churning up the foam of their shameful deeds" (Jude 1:12–13 NLT).

While they are hurting others, they are living a self-destructive lifestyle, and they themselves will eventually suffer most. Such lack of concern and loyalty eventually comes back to haunt them, wreaking havoc in their own lives and in the lives of their children, who are influenced by their lack of morals.

Responding to Betrayal

"Then many will be offended,
will betray one another, and will hate one another."
MATTHEW 24:10 NKJV

Chances are, someone whom you trusted has ended up betraying you. In a society dominated by self-centered attitudes, it is not surprising to see loyalties and friendships casually cast aside. It is a sign of the times, the steady deterioration of a once-moral society.

Jesus warned that in the last days many people would abandon their faith and would betray their former fellow believers. But how are you supposed to respond in such cases—and how should you react when someone betrays you for any reason?

Jesus gave the answer when He said, "Love your enemies, do good to those who hate you, bless those who curse you, and pray for those who spitefully use you" (Luke 6:27–28 NKJV). Yes, He expects you to forgive someone who has betrayed you, even if you can no longer trust that person and would no longer choose her or him as a confidant and friend.

It is important for your own sake that you forgive them. That way you keep your life free from bitterness and you are not carrying hatred around inside you.

Challenges

Eyes on God

"O our God, will You not judge them? For we have
no power. . .nor do we know what to do,
but our eyes are upon You."
2 CHRONICLES 20:12 NKJV

Christians are no strangers to problems. Sometimes it may seem that your life is *filled* with challenges, setbacks, and obstacles. At such times, you can only look to God and cry out, "Do not withhold Your tender mercies from me, O LORD. . . . For innumerable evils have surrounded me" (Psalm 40:11–12 NKJV).

These challenges could be opposition in the workplace, financial problems, serious long-term illnesses, or malicious people who seek to ruin your reputation.

In King Jehoshaphat's day, three enemy nations invaded Judah. They vastly outnumbered the Jews. Jehoshaphat and his people were overwhelmed. They had no idea what to do because there was nothing they could do. So they looked to God and cried out to Him.

God did a miracle to deliver them. And He can do the same for you today. He promises in His Word, "You will seek me and find me when you seek me with all your heart" (Jeremiah 29:13 NIV).

Relief from Attacks

*Be merciful to me, O God, for man would swallow
me up; fighting all day he oppresses me.*
PSALM 56:1 NKJV

Sometimes opponents are relentless in their attacks.
They get it into their heads that they should cause you
grief and therefore try everything they can think of to
oppose you. They keep at it day after day. That is when
you desperately need to pray for God to protect you.

Malicious busybodies can cause you a great deal
of pain when they take it on themselves to ruin your
reputation or get others to shun you. And when they
are popular or influential, their persecution amounts to
oppression. They may be either open or discreet about
their attacks, but the end result is the same.

David experienced this kind of oppression. Even
though he was the king of Israel, he had many powerful foes whose tongues secretly worked like razors
against him (Psalm 52:2). Read what he wrote in the
Psalms and you will draw great comfort from it.

While you can and should speak up to defend your
reputation and set the record straight, know that your
best defense is prayer. God will be a shield to you and
protect you.

But for God's Help

If it had not been the LORD who was on our side,
when men rose up against us: then they had
swallowed us up quick.
PSALM 124:2–3 KJV

If you think about it, you can probably remember times
when you came a hairbreadth away from disaster but
were spared. This includes traffic collisions or financial
calamity or times when vindictive people made you
their target. These close brushes happen all too often.

You may wonder why God allows such a barrage
of challenges. But it is the world and merciless enemies
that mount constant attrition against you, not God.
He steps in as your wall of protection, preventing the
ongoing attacks from sweeping you away.

Still, you may become weary of all this and worry
that one day God will fail to be there for you. David
wavered at one point. He had been pursued for years by
King Saul's armies and finally thought, "Someday Saul
is going to get me" (1 Samuel 27:1 NLT).

But it never happened. So don't give up before the
bell rings. God has your back. Stay faithful and He
won't allow your enemies to swallow you up.

Feeling Overwhelmed

*We were crushed and overwhelmed beyond our
ability to endure, and we thought we
would never live through it.*
2 CORINTHIANS 1:8 NLT

Paul and his fellow workers went through really
tough times. At one point, he candidly stated, "We
were crushed and overwhelmed beyond our ability to
endure." But you notice that he did endure, as did his
companions. But had the situation continued, they
wouldn't have.

God sometimes allows you to go through intol-
erable circumstances, that, if they lasted much longer,
would finish you. So Paul wasn't exaggerating when he
thought he might not make it. He actually wouldn't
have.

Some people harbor a niggling suspicion that God
is cruel for allowing believers to go through such severe
suffering and testing. But Paul put things in perspective when he said in that same epistle, "For our light
affliction, which is but for a moment, is working for
us a far more exceeding and eternal weight of glory" (2
Corinthians 4:17 NKJV).

What at the moment is an unendurable crushing
will be, in hindsight, "light affliction." You have to see
the troubles of this life in the light of heaven to arrive
at that conclusion.

Surviving Oppression

"Many a time they have afflicted me from my youth;
yet they have not prevailed against me."
PSALM 129:2 NKJV

Some people have been picked on for as long as they can remember. Ever since they were little, people bullied them because of some disability—or over their weight or some other physical feature. This was hard to bear, but they refused to succumb, no matter how discouraged they became.

"Those were the hard times! Kicked around in public, targets of every kind of abuse. . . . Nothing they did bothered you, nothing set you back" (Hebrews 10:33–34 MSG). Perhaps you suffered this way, and the memories of it often do bother you. Some people become introverted and depressed over such treatment and even develop suicidal tendencies.

But you survived and became more empathetic and compassionate toward others who also suffered from bullies. Perhaps, though you wouldn't care to repeat the experience, it even made you stronger.

Christian life is often similar. Paul says, "It has been granted to you on behalf of Christ not only to believe in him, but also to suffer for him" (Philippians 1:29 NIV).

Life Is Often Difficult

*"We must go through many hardships
to enter the kingdom of God."*
ACTS 14:22 NIV

Sometimes God calls you to bear the almost unbearable. You might be asked to endure prolonged financial insecurity, a debilitating illness, or family turmoil.

You may ask God why, but even more worrying, you ask yourself if God has abandoned you. But take heart in what one Hebrew psalmist declared: "You, who have shown me great and severe troubles, shall revive me again" (Psalm 71:20 NKJV).

If God plans on delivering you and has "plans to give you hope and a future" (Jeremiah 29:11 NIV), you may ask why He lets you experience such trouble in the first place. Well, He knows that as painful as these testings can be, good can come from them. He told the Jews: "I have refined you, but not as silver is refined. Rather, I have refined you in the furnace of suffering" (Isaiah 48:10 NLT).

Jesus said, "Narrow is the gate and difficult is the way which leads to life" (Matthew 7:14 NKJV). He promised that His followers would experience hardships. It's the price you must pay to walk as Jesus walked.

Chronic Illness

Sick for Years

She had suffered a great deal from many doctors,
and. . .spent everything she had to pay them,
but she had gotten no better.
MARK 5:26 NLT

There once was a woman who had a blood flow like a continual period. She had suffered for years, and despite seeking out the best physicians and spending all her savings on them, her suffering continued unabated.

Then she heard that Jesus, a holy man and healer, was in the city. But she couldn't ask Him to place His hands on her to heal her, for her condition made her ritually impure. Anyone who touched her would become "unclean." That is why she approached Him from behind and secretly touched His robe to tap in to His power. And she was healed.

Many people today have chronic illnesses as well. Like this woman, they suffer silently and in shame, convinced that their condition is a judgment from God. But the Lord looks down with eyes of love. "Jesus. . .had compassion on them and healed their sick" (Matthew 14:14 NIV).

Whether you find healing through physicians or the Great Physician, know that God loves you.

Sick a Long Time

One of the men lying there had been
sick for thirty-eight years.
JOHN 5:5 NLT

When you read the Gospels and see how often Jesus healed people, you get an idea of how many people were sick, had disabilities, or were suffering from infirmities. A huge percentage of society was sick, and some people had suffered chronic illnesses most of their lives. Think of the man at the Pool of Siloam. He had been bedridden for thirty-eight years.

The world's population is much greater today, and the number of sick people is also much greater. Chances are good that you know several people who suffer long-term illnesses or disabilities. The fact is, even churches who believe in healing have members who suffer on an ongoing basis.

Thank God when He heals people. And thank God for modern medicine that can also alleviate much suffering. But sometimes people suffer for years without a great deal of relief.

You really have to admire some people for how they manage to cope with limited health. They have learned both patience and humility. And while they long to be healed, they maintain a positive attitude through their condition.

Incurable, Evil Diseases

"An evil disease," they say, "clings to him.
And now that he lies down, he will rise up no more."
PSALM 41:8 NKJV

God warned the Israelites that if they persistently disobeyed Him, He would allow them to be afflicted with the evil diseases they had known in Egypt. "The LORD will afflict you with the boils of Egypt and with tumors, festering sores and the itch, from which you cannot be cured" (Deuteronomy 28:27 NIV).

Fast-forward to modern times: Not only is it discouraging to have an illness from which you can't be cured, but you are also left wondering what sin you committed. Now, some diseases are brought on by sin, and many are caused by unhealthy lifestyle choices, so you may be at fault—but not necessarily.

Even if so, the good news is that God can heal incurable, "evil" diseases. Although David's enemies were convinced that God was judging him and he was done for, David declared, "The LORD will strengthen him on his bed of illness; You will sustain him on his sickbed" (Psalm 41:3 NKJV). And God *did* heal him.

Chronic illnesses don't necessarily have to be forever.

Enduring Illness

My wound is incurable! Yet I said to myself,
"This is my sickness, and I must endure it."
JEREMIAH 10:19 NIV

Jeremiah warned his nation that if they didn't repent of their idolatry, God would send the Babylonians to conquer them. The Lord would give them many opportunities to repent, but He knew that they wouldn't, so their doom was sure. Jeremiah spoke for the nation, saying, "My wound is incurable!" He also knew that their judgment was just, so he said, "This is my sickness, and I must endure it."

Sometimes you will feel this same way if you have a chronic illness. God isn't necessarily judging you for some sin, however. You may simply be sick because you live in a fallen world and your physical body is susceptible to disease.

Certainly God can heal, and you do well to claim His promises and pray for a miracle. And if you have the faith and it is God's will, He will heal you. No disease is incurable to Him.

But if God *doesn't* heal you, you must have the fortitude to say, "This is my sickness, and I must endure it."

Severe Illnesses

Though his disease was severe. . .he did not seek help
from the LORD, but only from the physicians.
2 CHRONICLES 16:12 NIV

Doctors can now cure "incurable" diseases. For example, about 400 million people died from the Black Death in the 1300s. The mortality rate was in some places 95 percent. Cases of plague occasionally occur today, but the victims usually recover. And the list of medical marvels goes on and on.

You may have a chronic illness, and even though the newest experimental medicines can't completely cure it, they may go a long way to making it manageable.

It's wise to see a doctor when you are sick, and the Bible doesn't indicate that believers are to seek only miraculous healing. But there is still much that even the best doctors don't know. So while consulting them, you must also look to the Lord. He is the ultimate Healer.

King Asa looked for help only from physicians and failed to seek God—even when his disease became severe. As a result, he died. This is not to "dis" modern medicine, however, but simply to remind you to look to God.

Chronic Pain

Suffering Infirmity in Old Age

*Elisha had been suffering
from the illness from which he died.*
2 KINGS 13:14 NIV

Elisha had great faith for healing miracles. Once a boy became so sick that he died, but when Elisha prayed for him, he came back to life. Yet when Elisha himself was advanced in years, he became very ill, and instead of being healed, he became so sick that he died. And he didn't come back to life.

The Bible doesn't tell what Elisha's medical condition was—whether cancer, MS, or tuberculosis—but he apparently suffered for some time. He very likely wondered, *Lord, I've served You faithfully all my life. Why are You letting me suffer like this?"*

Often, even righteous, obedient people must endure debilitating diseases. You may have hoped to live to a ripe old age and to be in excellent health right till the end, just like Moses (Deuteronomy 34:7). But life may turn out differently.

Understanding why God allows such infirmities is difficult. But one day everything will be clear, and you will understand. In the meantime, God offers you the grace to be "patient in trouble" (Romans 12:12 NLT).

Relentless Pain

"At night my bones are filled with pain,
which gnaws at me relentlessly."
JOB 30:17 NLT

Sometimes you feel pain that defies medical description. Even though Job had broken no bones, the throbbing pain felt like he had. During his ordeal, he said, "Man is also chastened with pain on his bed, and with strong pain in many of his bones" (Job 33:19 NKJV).

God has loving purposes for chastening people. He says, "Those whom I love I rebuke and discipline. So be earnest and repent" (Revelation 3:19 NIV). Scripture admits that this process can be difficult: "No discipline seems pleasant at the time, but painful. Later on, however, it produces. . .righteousness and peace for those who have been trained by it" (Hebrews 12:11 NIV).

God designed our nerves to feel pain. Pain is necessary. If you felt no pain when you put your hand on a stove, you'd be badly burned. Instead, you jerk quickly away, thanks to your pain sensors. Christians learn many valuable lessons through pain, though the learning is difficult.

Jesus Also Suffered

He was despised and rejected by mankind,
a man of suffering, and familiar with pain.
ISAIAH 53:3 NIV

When you suffer from chronic pain, it is easy to think that God is distant and uncaring. Like David, you may ask, "Why do You stand afar off, O LORD? Why do You hide in times of trouble?" (Psalm 10:1 NKJV). But God knows what you are going through. He says, "I know their sorrows" (Exodus 3:7 NKJV).

The Bible calls Jesus "a man of suffering, and familiar with pain" (Isaiah 53:3 NIV). He suffered unbelievable pain during the hours He endured scourging and crucifixion. But Jesus had suffered grief and psychological pain for years. "He came to his own people, and even they rejected him" (John 1:11 NLT). He frequently lamented, "O faithless and perverse generation, how long. . .shall I bear with you?" (Matthew 17:17 NKJV), and He was "grieved for the hardness of their hearts" (Mark 3:5 KJV).

Jesus was "familiar with pain," and this is not merely an expression. He understands what constant suffering is like, and He will be with you in your pain and lonely hours when no one else seems to care.

Focused on Pain

They feel but the pain of their own bodies
and mourn only for themselves.
JOB 14:22 NIV

Job was speaking for millions of people when he said,
"They feel but the pain of their own bodies and mourn
only for themselves." Most people who experience
chronic pain are focused on their own suffering. And
this is to be expected. When you are in constant dis-
comfort and pain, you may find it difficult to concentrate on anything else.

You may be aware that many other people in this
world are suffering as much as you—some even more
so—but you may feel you have enough to think about
already, just dealing with your own misery. No one
should judge you for thinking that way if you are experiencing chronic pain.

On the other hand, your suffering should give you
compassion for others who are suffering also. You of
all people know how they feel and are in a position to
comfort them, as well as to give them advice to alleviate their pain. So reach out today to someone who, like
you, is suffering. That person will appreciate it, and it
will do your heart good.

Church Discord

Euodia and Syntyche

*I plead with Euodia and I plead with Syntyche
to be of the same mind in the Lord.*
PHILIPPIANS 4:2 NIV

Paul had a deep love for the believers of Philippi. They had endured great persecution for their faith. They were generous and had faithfully supported his ministry. But he had to pause his praise at one point to give a shout-out to two women: Euodia ("sweet fragrance") and Syntyche ("fortunate"), who were allowing their disagreements to disrupt the church.

These were not two unspiritual busybodies, the kind of idle troublemakers you would expect to be involved in dissension. They were prominent women, companions of Paul, both active in God's work. In the next breath, Paul implores a church leader, "I ask you. . .help these women since they have contended at my side in the cause of the gospel" (Philippians 4:3 NIV).

Even the best of us sometimes collide with other believers, and at such times, may need help from spiritual leaders to sort out our quarrels. We won't always agree on all points, but we should "be of the same mind" regarding important issues such as love and unity.

Harmony and Peace

Encourage each other. Live in harmony and peace.
Then the God of love and peace will be with you.
2 CORINTHIANS 13:11 NLT

Paul states an important fact: God is the "God of love and peace." You are probably already familiar with the famous statement that "God is love" (1 John 4:8 KJV), but it is important to realize that He is also the Spirit of peace. Whenever God is, there is peace.

Jesus said, "Where two or three are gathered together in My name, I am there in the midst of them" (Matthew 18:20 NKJV). Since Jesus is one with God the Father, where He is there is love and peace. This peace should be in evidence whenever Christians come together in His name. So it is only natural that believers encourage one another and live in harmony and tranquility.

Discord in the church could be avoided if Christians recognized that Jesus is personally present when they gather to worship, to hear the Word, and to fellowship. They must realize that the same Spirit of Christ present in their own life is present in other believers. To respect others is to respect Jesus.

Rebelling in Pride

I wrote to the church, but Diotrephes, who loves to
have the preeminence among them, does not receive us.
3 JOHN 1:9 NKJV

Often church discord is caused by nothing but pride. In his later years, the apostle John was based in Ephesus and oversaw the churches in the surrounding cities. Most Christians respected this great apostle and gladly listened to his instructions and admonitions.

But John was a simple man with a simple message, and getting along in years—and a few local elders resented having to submit to him. They were well-to-do, educated, and eloquent, and used to people respecting *them*. They loved being preeminent in their little kingdoms.

Unfortunately, some people today are like Diotrephes, and their pride causes problems and schisms in the church. But this isn't exceptional. We should all check our hearts: If we even have a slight touch of that attitude, it can cause us to resent godly leadership.

The Bible instructs us, "Have confidence in your leaders and submit to their authority, because they keep watch over you" (Hebrews 13:17 NIV). Be on guard against pride that would make you think you can ignore spiritual leaders.

Carnal Divisions

Whereas there is among you envying, and strife,
and divisions, are ye not carnal, and walk as men?
1 CORINTHIANS 3:3 KJV

A number of churches are plagued by doctrinal disagreements; people envy each other's jobs and positions; and strife, discord, and competition abound. Sometimes the divisions come out in the open as church splits. While people may give scriptural motives for their actions, often the reason is that they are simply lacking in love.

As Paul told the Corinthians, though they had experienced the life-changing power of God's Spirit, they were acting like carnal, unregenerate people who had never known God. So Paul advised them, "If we live in the Spirit, let us also walk in the Spirit" (Galatians 5:25 KJV). Let what is in your heart be made manifest in your outward actions.

Since "the love of God has been poured out in our hearts by the Holy Spirit" (Romans 5:5 NKJV), you should yield to the Holy Spirit and walk in that love. How do you avoid strife, divisions, and envy? "Walk in the Spirit, and you shall not fulfill the lust of the flesh" (Galatians 5:16 NKJV).

Necessary Disputes

*This brought Paul and Barnabas into sharp
dispute and debate with them.*
Acts 15:2 niv

Usually when disputes arise in a church, they are over doctrinal issues, church practices, or finances. Some people get stirred up emotionally and get argumentative over issues, while others want to just soothe the troubled waters and make all disagreements go away.

Some debates, however, are necessary. Certain doctrines are just plain wrong, many practices are inappropriate, and some financial decisions, if followed, would prove disastrous. But it is important to debate the issues in a loving manner and respectful tone, not in pride and anger, not impugning others' integrity or mocking their intelligence.

When certain Jews preached that Gentile believers had to become circumcised and keep Moses' law to be saved, Paul and Barnabas had a "sharp dispute and debate" with them. And they were right to do so. Jude advised Christians to "earnestly contend for the faith" (Jude 1:3 kjv).

But it is important that it is the issues that are sharply defined, not that the tones of voices are sharp. Even in a heated debate, Christians must be found "speaking the truth in love" (Ephesians 4:15 kjv).

Death of a Child

Mourning a Child

*"While the child was alive,
I fasted and wept. . . . But now he is dead."*
2 SAMUEL 12:22–23 NKJV

David had a child by Bathsheba, but he had committed adultery with her and had her husband murdered, so God told him that the child would die. When the infant became sick, David fasted and wept. But because God had made His will clear, David accepted the fact when the baby passed away.

Usually, however, the reasons for a child's death aren't clear, and you are left in grief, wondering why God took him or her. Losing a child is a very painful experience. It's almost never a consequence of your sin, but you may feel that God has acted cruelly or without reason.

It's often easier to accept the death of a parent who has lived a full life than it is to see a child die before having an opportunity to experience what life on earth has to offer. One question burns in your mind: "*Why?*" And there usually doesn't seem to be an acceptable answer.

God understands your grief. But He also knows that you will have great joy when you are reunited with your child in heaven.

When Your Child Dies

Some time later the woman's son became sick.
He grew worse and worse, and finally he died.
1 Kings 17:17 NLT

Many a parent has passed sleepless nights watching over a child with a terminal illness. You endure agony as you watch them pass "through the valley of the shadow of death" (Psalm 23:4 KJV). And the pain is overwhelming when he or she finally leaves this life.

It's very difficult to say good-bye. And the days that follow have even more pain. You sit silently in his room, trying to grasp that he is truly gone. You arrange her toy animals on her bed, as if that might somehow make some sense of all the pain.

But try as you might, it makes no sense. What could be the purpose in taking such a beautiful child? But just as with Enoch, God has His reasons. "Enoch lived in close fellowship with God. . . . Then one day. . .God took him" (Genesis 5:22, 24 NLT).

Only time will heal your heartache—that and the knowledge that your child is now running through bright fields of splendor above, totally, unreservedly happy.

Jairus's Daughter

Weep not; she is not dead, but sleepeth.
LUKE 8:52 KJV

We all eventually die, and when someone's time has come to leave this life, we do well to accept it. But that isn't easy when the person whose time has come is very young and hasn't yet experienced all that life has to offer.

The New Testament records Jesus raising the dead on three occasions: He revived a young man; He brought a twelve-year-old girl back to life; and He raised his friend Lazarus (Luke 7:14–15; 8:51–55; John 11:38–44). Raising the dead was an exception, even for Jesus. Many hundreds of people died in Israel during the time of Jesus' ministry, and they didn't return.

But when someone dies with faith in Jesus, they live forever in His heavenly kingdom. This life is not the end, and the Bible refers to their temporary absence as "sleeping" (1 Corinthians 15:51; 1 Thessalonians 4:14). One day God will wake them, and their physical bodies will be resurrected in eternal life.

In that day, you and your departed child shall live together once again in rapturous joy.

With You a Short Time

*"Never again will there be in it an infant
who lives but a few days."*
ISAIAH 65:20 NIV

Jesus once described a woman suffering the pains of labor: "When her child is born, her anguish gives way to joy because she has brought a new baby into the world" (John 16:21 NLT). After nine months of pregnancy, parents are delighted to welcome a new life.

But sometimes that joy is short-lived. Even though the infant mortality rate is very low in the West, children still die in their first months. This raises painful questions: Why was this new life given, only to be snatched away? And the inevitable question: What did I do wrong?

It's usually not that you did anything wrong. God isn't judging you for some sin. It's just that life is often hard. People in developing nations face this grim reality on a much more frequent basis. But one day such sorrow will be no more in all the earth.

During the coming reign of Christ on earth, "the child shall die one hundred years old" after living a full, happy life (Isaiah 65:20 NKJV).

Death of a Parent

The Passing of a Parent

I bowed down heavily,
as one who mourns for his mother.
PSALM 35:14 NKJV

No matter how many signs you have of a parent's approaching death, even if he or she has been in failing health for years, the time of death can still come as a shock. It's the finality of it—knowing that you will never hear your father tell another corny joke or your mother express joy over another simple gift.

The grandfather's clock still ticks away, but your parent's chair is now empty. Everywhere you look you find memories—from the photo albums, to the pictures on the walls, to the unfinished woodworking projects in his garage or the half-knitted sweater in her sitting room.

Your mind is numb, and it takes the actual funeral for the reality to sink in that your parent is gone. Your days are filled with kind faces and gentle voices speaking condolences, but with every night come the emptiness and the tears.

You know your parent is with God now, and you know that must be incredibly beautiful, but you still need time to deal with your grief.

On to a Heavenly Reward

Then he breathed his last and died at a ripe old age,
joining his ancestors in death.
GENESIS 35:29 NLT

Isaac lived to a great age, and when he passed away, his sons Esau and Jacob came to bury him. All his household mourned him. But Isaac had died "at a ripe old age," having lived a long, eventful life for God. The passing of this great man was as much an occasion to celebrate his legacy as it was to mourn his death.

Isaac had been fading for years—likely for decades—so his death came as no surprise. The passing away of your parents may be similar. They may even have had "a desire to depart and be with Christ" (Philippians 1:23 NKJV).

In fact, since Jesus opened the way to heaven, the demise of any born-again senior saint is cause for celebration. Although you will certainly miss your loved ones, it is comforting to know that if they loved the Lord they have gone on to a well-deserved reward. It's wonderful to realize that they are finally home, thronged by a company of great saints of ages past who have gone there before them.

Grieving a Mother

He married Rebekah and. . .he loved her.
So Isaac found comfort after his mother's death.
GENESIS 24:67 MSG

When Sarah died, Abraham mourned and wept bitter tears. But Abraham wasn't the only one in mourning. His son Isaac also grieved. He was the only son of his mother, and they'd had a special bond. So for months after her death, he found no comfort.

Abraham took another wife named Keturah, and he wisely realized that it was time that his son got married. So he sent a servant to Haran, and soon Rebekah came riding back in the camel caravan. After he was married, Isaac found solace, sweet companionship, and a sympathetic ear in Rebekah.

When your mother dies, you will probably feel emptiness within—even if you weren't as close to her as Isaac was to his mother. And though life must go on, there may be a mantle of grief draped over your days for some time.

Be sure to reach out to others who understand your sorrow and can sympathize and weep with you (Romans 12:15). It's important to process your grief, not bottle it all up inside.

A Ripe Sheaf of Grain

"You shall come to the grave at a full age,
as a sheaf of grain ripens in its season."
JOB 5:26 NKJV

A long life lived for God is a beautiful thing. The departure to heaven of an aged saint is a joyful event. For when they finally arrive in their eternal home, they will hear, "Well done, good and faithful servant" (Matthew 25:21 NKJV).

The Bible describes the death of a senior saint in delightful terms: If they die at a "full age," crowned with a head of white hair, scripture says they are like a sheaf of grain that has ripened at the end of the long summer season. Then the long-awaited harvest comes and they are taken home. Of course, their passing is bittersweet for those left behind, but death for a Christian is not the end.

It's right and proper to mourn the passing of an elderly believer, but it is also appropriate to celebrate a life well lived and to focus on the legacy the person leaves. This is true even if the person didn't accomplish "great" things but was simply a faithful husband or wife and a loving grandparent.

Death of a Pet

One Little Ewe Lamb

*"The poor man had nothing except one little
ewe lamb. . . . It was like a daughter to him."*
2 SAMUEL 12:3 NIV

A prophet once told David a story about a man who
kept a lamb as a house pet. "He raised it, and it grew
up with him and his children. It shared his food, drank
from his cup and even slept in his arms. It was like a
daughter to him" (2 Samuel 12:3 NIV). David was overcome with emotion when he learned that the lamb had
been killed.

People have had tender feelings for pets for thousands of years and have felt keen grief when they die.
Some modern people shake their head in disbelief
when their grieving mother laments the death of her
dog. But God created animals capable of expressing
affection, and He understands.

Do animals go to heaven? Many may do so. Revelation 19:11, 14 tell us there are horses in paradise.
And Isaiah 65:17, 25 describes animals such as wolves,
sheep, lions, cattle, and snakes there. Dogs aren't specifically mentioned, but we can safely assume that if
wolves are there, dogs will be there as well.

A Four-Footed Friend

"Even the little dogs eat the crumbs which
fall from their masters' table."
MATTHEW 15:27 NKJV

Dogs weren't looked on with much fondness in ancient Israel. Although some served as sheepdogs, most were simply strays wandering the streets of the city in packs, foraging through garbage, growling at people who got too close. So the Old Testament doesn't share a great deal of tender sentiments about dogs.

But by New Testament times, they had been fully accepted as pets, were often small breeds like the "little dogs" referred to in Matthew 15:27, and had made their way into people's hearts and homes. They frequently lay under the table at their masters' feet, eating the scraps that dropped. A Phoenician woman made reference of this fact to Jesus.

Dogs experience love, happiness, and other emotions just like people, and as they develop closer bonds, each often mourns the other's passing. Dogs experience genuine grief when their masters die, and people often feel pangs of sorrow when their dogs die.

Don't be ashamed to grieve when your four-footed companion passes away. God has a tender spot in His heart for His creations as well.

Death of a Spouse

Loss of a Partner

Then Elimelech died,
and Naomi was left with her two sons.
RUTH 1:3 NLT

Once when there was a long famine in Israel, Naomi and her husband sold their land to buy food; then they left Bethlehem for Moab, where they found some relief for a few years. There Naomi's husband died. Naomi was grief-stricken, and none of her relatives and former neighbors were present to comfort her.

To make matters worse, her two sons died also. This left her financially destitute. A devastated widow, she decided to return to Israel. As she went, she lamented, "The LORD's hand has turned against me!" (Ruth 1:13 NIV).

Many people down through the centuries have identified with Naomi's feelings of despair. It is very difficult to lose a life partner. And it is worse when you have to take over your deceased spouse's duties and handle the finances.

But we know the end of Naomi's story: God showed her tender compassion. Her daughter-in-law Ruth had returned with her to Judah, married a wealthy landowner, and cared for her. Naomi had thought that God had abandoned her. . .but He hadn't. He hasn't abandoned you either.

Mourning a Life Companion

Sarah died. . .and Abraham came to mourn
for Sarah, and to weep for her.
GENESIS 23:2 KJV

Sarah lived for 127 years, so she and Abraham had been married for about 110 years. Sarah was very beautiful and maintained her lovely features into her senior years. We know this because the king of Gerar desired to marry her even when she was ninety (Genesis 17:17; 20:1–2).

When Sarah died, Abraham wept openly. She had been his closest companion for over a century. Then, cloaked in his grief, he took care of funeral arrangements. It was at this time that he bought the cave of Machpelah for a family tomb.

When your life's companion dies, it seems that part of you dies as well. You had "become one" in marriage, and your physical beings, emotions, and habits had become almost inextricably intertwined, so much so that you can be at a loss as to how you will cope. This is different from the loss of a friend or even a family member.

At such times, the knowledge that you will see your loved one again in heaven gives steady light for your path.

The Desire of Your Eyes

"Behold, I take away from you the desire
of your eyes with one stroke."
EZEKIEL 24:16 NKJV

Ezekiel was a young priest, and like many other Jewish captives, he was living in exile in Babylon. But he had one consolation: He was very happily married and his wife was "the desire of his eyes." Then one morning God warned Ezekiel that He was about to take her.

The Bible doesn't indicate whether Ezekiel's wife was already sick from a lingering disease—and whether she took a turn for the worse, prompting this revelation—or whether she suffered from a sudden, unexpected stroke. But that same evening she died.

God gave Ezekiel a very unusual command, instructing him not to mourn outwardly, but to "sigh in silence" (24:17 NKJV). And Ezekiel obeyed. If his wife had been sick for many months, this would have given him time to prepare for her eventual demise, but still, Ezekiel would have been very heavyhearted.

It is especially difficult when your spouse dies young, in the prime of life. God understands your sorrow and expects you to grieve. His command to Ezekiel was a rare exception.

Depression

Refusing to Despair

We are pressed on every side by troubles, but we are not crushed. We are perplexed, but not driven to despair.
2 CORINTHIANS 4:8 NLT

The apostle Paul endured unbelievable hardships yet kept a positive outlook. In Philippi, he and Silas were cruelly beaten and thrown into prison. Instead of complaining, they sang praise to God (Acts 16:22–25). Paul refused to give in to despair and later advised the persecuted Philippian believers, "Rejoice in the Lord always. Again I will say, rejoice!" (Philippians 4:4 NKJV).

Many modern Christians, however, suffer from depression, and though they battle it and seek to stay positive, they are not always successful. Instead of berating them for being too weak to maintain a victorious attitude, we should commend them for their efforts and encourage them to continue trusting God.

If you suffer from clinical depression, you may sometimes feel helpless to rise above dark waves of depression. Don't feel condemned if you need to take medication to adjust a chemical imbalance in your brain.

At the same time, aggressively strive to be positive—soaking your thoughts in God's Word, listening to praise and worship music, and constantly quoting faith-building promises from scripture.

Reason to Live

"What strength do I have, that I should hope?
And what is my end, that I should prolong my life?"
JOB 6:11 NKJV

Depression can have many causes, but when it comes, it can sap your will to live. You don't feel like doing anything. Everything seems hopeless. And sometimes there may not be much you can do—particularly if you have a physical disability that leaves you with little strength or bedridden.

You may wonder why you should continue to hope. What strength do you have to act even if an opportunity were to open? What is God's plan, what end does He have in mind, that you should continue hoping? What could He possibly still have for you to accomplish, given the state you are in?

If you feel there is no reason to live, you may desire to depart for heaven before God is done with you on earth. But God doesn't see the way people see. What to you may seem like large, meaningful accomplishments—causes well worth living for—may have little significance to God. But small, everyday acts that seem almost insignificant to you may be vitally important to Him.

A Crushed Spirit

My heart is smitten, and withered like grass;
so that I forget to eat my bread.
PSALM 102:4 KJV

You can bear up under great adversity as long as you have hope. You can suffer setbacks and sicknesses or endure rejection as long as you keep your spirits up. But once you lose hope, you succumb to depression. "The human spirit can endure in sickness, but a crushed spirit who can bear?" (Proverbs 18:14 NIV).

The Bible tells us that "a broken spirit dries the bones" (Proverbs 17:22 NKJV). Sometimes you feel hopeless and dispirited. And when this happens, you have no will to continue. You are unable to go on.

If you are suffering from depression, the source of your pain may be a broken spirit. Life has battered you badly, shaking your trust in God, and drained your will to continue. And if you had a preexisting disposition to depression, it has hit you all the harder.

Rest in the Lord and let Him renew you. Meditate on His Word and draw strength from His promises. Allow His gentle hands to mend your wounds and restore your confidence.

A Broken Spirit

The spirit of a man will sustain him in sickness,
but who can bear a broken spirit?
PROVERBS 18:14 NKJV

If you have faith in God, it will keep you going even when you are sick. But if you lose all hope, if your spirit is weak and broken, nothing remains to sustain you. Then you are left with depression.

Many Christians mistakenly think that God wants them to be desperate, broken, and weeping, for they wrongly translate David's words, "The LORD is close to the brokenhearted and saves those who are crushed in spirit" (Psalm 34:18 NIV). However, He draws near you to heal your broken spirit and comfort you—not to make you broken.

Throughout the Scriptures, being broken means being shattered (Jeremiah 19:1–2, 10–11) and crushed and weak (Proverbs 15:13; 17:22). Breaking is what happens to dry, brittle, hardened vessels that can no longer be changed, for whom there is no more hope.

But if you are a moist, soft clay vessel, still trusting God, still on the Potter's wheel, He allows pressure to mold and shape you. This pressure may be painful at times, but it leads to godly change, not hopelessness and depression.

A Comforting Friend

*It was a beautiful thing that you came
alongside me in my troubles.*
PHILIPPIANS 4:14 MSG

Many people don't have an actual case of clinical depression; nevertheless, they feel down and depressed. Perhaps life has dealt them a series of hard blows that have dampened their spirits and weighed them down. Or perhaps there is a cloud over their days because of worries about their health, their finances, or their families.

Taking the time to speak encouraging words to them can be a huge help. Solomon said, "Anxiety in the heart of man causes depression, but a good word makes it glad" (Proverbs 12:25 NKJV).

You may hesitate to try to encourage someone. You may think that you won't know what to say, that you will come off sounding awkward, or that your words won't have any effect. Go ahead and do it anyway. Your friend will probably appreciate that you cared enough to try.

Sometimes just coming alongside someone helps, even if you don't have great words of wisdom to impart. They will be glad to know that you are thinking about them and praying for them.

Disabilities

When Children Have Disabilities

His nurse picked him up and fled, but as she hurried to leave, he fell and became disabled.
2 SAMUEL 4:4 NIV

It's difficult to understand why babies are born with disabilities. It's just as difficult to understand why God allows young children to suffer disease or accidents that leave them disabled for life. This causes parents to ask, "Why *her*, God? What did this innocent child ever do to deserve this?"

The answer is that the child didn't "deserve" it, but diseases and accidents are no respecters of persons, and even children aren't spared. So they are born blind, deaf, and disabled, and while this causes the parents grief and soul-searching at first, they eventually accept their children's limitations and learn to encourage them to reach their full potential just the same.

But don't forget: God will one day utterly change them. Their present bodies may be weak or disabled, but when His kingdom comes, their bodies will be transformed and made powerful and eternal. "Our bodies are buried in brokenness, but they will be raised in glory. They are buried in weakness, but they will be raised in strength" (1 Corinthians 15:43 NLT).

Caring for Those with Disabilities

*"When you give a banquet, invite the poor, the crippled,
the lame, the blind, and you will be blessed."*
LUKE 14:13–14 NIV

You may observe people gently caring for those with
physical or mental disabilities, and think, *So much love!
I could never do that.* You may admire their dedication
but not be able to imagine rolling up your sleeves and
caring for those with disabilities yourself.

But caring for the poor, the disabled, the lame, the
blind, and the mentally challenged can often be part
of living the Gospel. Jesus cares for them, and He tells
those of us who follow Him to help the disadvantaged:
"Whenever you did one of these things to someone
overlooked or ignored, that was me—you did it to me"
(Matthew 25:40 MSG).

Such loving actions begin at home—caring for
a family member with disabilities, feeding an elderly
parent, spending time talking with a shut-in relative
who tells you the same stories every time you visit.

If you yourself are disabled, you know how much
such care and acts of kindness mean. So go the extra
mile and show the same love to those less fortunate
than you.

Levites with Disabilities

"No man who has any defect may come near:
no man who is blind or lame, disfigured or deformed."
LEVITICUS 21:18 NIV

The law of Moses stated that no Levite who was "blind or lame, disfigured or deformed" could offer food to God on His altar. Some readers therefore conclude that God thinks less of those with disabilities, and they wonder why a God of love would reject the human beings with disabilities whom He Himself formed.

But God's love and care extend to those with disabilities, for in the same passage, the Lord said, "He may eat the most holy food of his God, as well as the holy food; yet because of his defect, he must not. . .approach the altar" (Leviticus 21:22–23 NIV).

Levites with disabilities could eat the food dedicated to God Almighty, including "the most holy food"—which was off-limits to the vast majority of Israelites. God did not care less for them just because they weren't permitted to do everything able-bodied Levites did.

And now that Christ has opened the way to the Father, this restriction is past, and God's disabled children freely approach His throne of grace.

Healing and Helping

He looked up and said,
"I see men like trees, walking."
MARK 8:24 NKJV

When Jesus came to Bethsaida, people brought a blind man to Him. Instead of immediately healing him, Jesus led him away from the crowds. Then He spit on his eyes, placed His hands on him, and asked him if he saw anything.

The man replied, "I see men like trees, walking." So Jesus placed His hands on the man's eyes again and made him look up. This time he saw everyone clearly. These days if someone saw men that blurry, most Christians would refer him to the optometrist.

In fact, medical missionaries, lacking the ability to miraculously heal the visually impaired, equip them with glasses or perform eye operations to correct their vision. And instead of healing paraplegics, practical Christians motivated by love provide wheelchairs to give them mobility.

It's great if you have the faith to heal the blind, the paralyzed, and the disabled, but few Christians actually have faith like that. But we should all have the love of Christ. And remember, it is even more important to have love than the faith to work miracles (1 Corinthians 13:2, 13).

God's Children with Disabilities

"Who makes the mute, the deaf, the seeing,
or the blind? Have not I, the LORD?"
EXODUS 4:11 NKJV

You may have proclaimed this verse when a baby was born: "I praise you because I am fearfully and wonderfully made; your works are wonderful" (Psalm 139:14 NIV). But are God's works still wonderful when a child is born blind or with another imperfection? Yes, they are.

You may wonder what purpose the Lord has in creating the mute, the deaf, and the blind. But you do well to remember that all human beings are imperfect in one way or another—often in many ways. What is God's purpose in creating us?

Well, our lives owe much of their significance to how we affect others. People with disabilities have a powerful effect on people. They present countless opportunities to others to show compassion. When you love and help others, you fulfill Christ's law. "Carry each other's burdens, and in this way you will fulfill the law of Christ" (Galatians 6:2 NIV).

When we get to heaven, we will see how backward we had so many of our priorities, for "the last shall be first" (Matthew 19:30 KJV).

Disappointment

Unrelenting Disappointment

Unrelenting disappointment leaves you heartsick,
but a sudden good break can turn life around.
PROVERBS 13:12 MSG

God knows that relentless disappointment leaves you mentally exhausted. After a while, you begin to get the feeling that nothing good will ever come your way again. You are overcome with futility.

You may feel like Job, whose friends tried to encourage him that if he would hang in there, just persevere, that God would eventually bless him again (Job 4:3–7; 8:6, 21). God would "restore to you the years that the. . .locust has eaten" (Joel 2:25 NKJV).

But like Job, you may have nearly given up hope that this will ever happen. When the locusts have devoured so many years of your life and you are persuaded that God Himself is intent on causing you grief, it is difficult to think that it will ever seem like a good idea to Him to bless you again.

But this time of testing and disappointment won't last forever. It, too, will pass. God loves you and is determined to do good in your life. Like the sun bursting through the clouds, He will completely change your situation and give you hope again.

Dealing with Disappointment

"The brook vanishes in the heat. The caravans turn aside to be refreshed, but there is nothing to drink."
JOB 6:17–18 NLT

In Bible lands, intermittent brooks—called *wadis*—run with water only after the spring rains. Then, as the long, hot summer months stretch on, the streambeds dry up. Soon water is to be found only in a few small pools. Many a caravan has stopped at a *wadi*, desperate for water, to find nothing at all.

Perhaps you have experienced similar disappointment: You were depending on a job to come through. You had exhausted all your other resources and had no backup plan. You needed this to happen. Yet it fell through, and you were bitterly disheartened.

What can you do? The Bible describes the arid valley of Baca. *Baca* means "weeping" and symbolizes times of great disappointment. Yet God's people "passing through the valley of Baca make it a well" (Psalm 84:6 KJV). When you desperately need water but there is none in sight, that is when you must dig a well.

God will never fail you, but sometimes you need to dig deep in a place of disappointment to find hope.

When Hopes Are Dashed

They count on it but are disappointed.
When they arrive, their hopes are dashed.
JOB 6:20 NLT

When you are counting on someone to help you but the time comes and your would-be helper bails out, your hopes are dashed. Maybe he promised to lend you money to meet an unexpected shortfall, or she said she would drive you to an appointment, but then the person doesn't come through.

God knows what it is like to be disappointed. He compared His care for Israel to a farmer painstakingly preparing the ground, removing stones, and planting a vineyard. Yet the vine produced bitter grapes. God asked, "What more could have been done to My vineyard that I have not done in it? Why then, when I expected it to bring forth good grapes, did it bring forth wild grapes?" (Isaiah 5:4 NKJV).

People continue to disappoint God today, yet He patiently, lovingly continues to work in their lives. "For He knows our frame; He remembers that we are dust" (Psalm 103:14 NKJV).

When your hopes fall through, look to God to comfort you and meet your needs. He will come through for you when people fail.

Hope That Never Disappoints

This hope will not lead to disappointment.
For we know how dearly God loves us.
ROMANS 5:5 NLT

We all have had high hopes at times and have had our hearts set on something, only to be disappointed. People forget their promises or thoughtlessly fail to keep their word, and even "sure deals" fall through. Problems and trials seem to be woven right into the fabric of life and are constantly upsetting our carefully made plans.

But Paul said that it is not only possible to endure when you run into problems, but to rejoice, because trials develop godly character. This development process strengthens your confident hope of salvation, and such hope will never lead to disappointment.

Sometimes it is helpful to take a deep breath, pause for a moment, and see disappointments in perspective. This life is full of frustrations and failures, but through them all, God works everything for good and will more than make up for your losses in heaven.

You can be certain of this, knowing how much God loves you. This love is what moves Him to have so many wonderful things planned and waiting for you. And God never disappoints.

Disappointing Returns

"You looked for much, but indeed it came to little."
HAGGAI 1:9 NKJV

How many times have you launched out on a new venture with high hopes, only to have your hopes dashed? Many times, if you are an entrepreneur. This can be very upsetting after putting your all into something.

You realize that in the past you have gone off half-cocked, so this time you do lots of research, come up with a truly winning idea, and carefully plan all the details—only to fail again.

As the prophet Haggai explained, this often happens if you don't put God and His purposes first. As a result, He isn't with you to bless you. But it can also happen for inscrutable marketing reasons, and often there is no way to accurately predict what will succeed. The Bible says, "For you do not know which will prosper, either this or that" (Ecclesiastes 11:6 NKJV).

As Solomon noted, "The race is not to the swift. . .nor riches to men of understanding, nor favor to men of skill; but time and chance happen to them all" (Ecclesiastes 9:11 NKJV). Often that is just the way things are.

Dishonesty

Live Honestly

Live in the fear of GOD—be most careful,
for GOD hates dishonesty, partiality, and bribery.
2 CHRONICLES 19:7 MSG

Human nature is predictable: it always seeks comfort, pleasure, and plenty, and avoids difficulty, pain, and loss. That is why people are so often tempted to cut corners at work or to fudge numbers when charging customers or paying taxes. Sometimes it seems that dishonesty is the default setting of mankind.

Partiality is another way of bending the rules. While you may be convinced that you treat everyone the same, do you show favorites by allowing certain people privileges, access, and leniency that you don't offer to others?

And while you might be dismayed at the blatant bribery in Third World countries, it is nevertheless alive (in its more polite forms) in our own country. For example, are you more inclined to do things promptly and well for people who have shown favors to you or scratched your back in some way?

The best way to avoid dishonesty and partiality is to revere God and seek to please Him. Then He will help you to be honest in all your dealings with others.

Honesty and Dishonesty

Honesty guides good people;
dishonesty destroys treacherous people.
PROVERBS 11:3 NLT

Picture yourself traveling through unfamiliar territory in the dark. The path has many forks, and you have no idea which way to choose. Would you be happy if someone who knows that region like the back of his hand offered to guide you to your destination? Of course!

Life itself is often dark, unfamiliar territory. But you can know that you are walking on the right path if you have honesty guiding your steps.

Many times, if you choose what is honest, you seem to be losing out—while unscrupulous, crooked people who take devious shortcuts get ahead in life. But you avoid many pitfalls by having integrity. For one thing, if you both get audited, he is the one who suffers.

And if you consistently own up to your mistakes instead of trying to wiggle out of any responsibility, you will gain a reputation for honesty. This will serve you well.

It may take a while, sometimes years, but dishonesty eventually destroys those foolish enough to indulge in it. "Better to be poor and honest than to be dishonest and a fool" (Proverbs 19:1 NLT).

Principles of Honesty

*Whoever is dishonest with very little will
also be dishonest with much.*
LUKE 16:10 NIV

How you handle dimes and dollars is a very good indicator of how you will handle a much larger amount. You might think that small sums of money aren't significant—it is all slush fund until it reaches a certain threshold. But God watches how honest you are with pocket change before He trusts you with more.

The aggregate effect of small, corrupt money habits carries a huge price tag. Even a small hole will eventually sink a large ship. The continual dripping of a leaky faucet will, over time, drain your tank dry. And as Solomon put it, "the little foxes. . .ruin the vineyards" (Song of Songs 2:15 NIV).

Besides, if you are used to spending money recklessly and aren't on the level with small sums, your habits will continue unchanged if you come into a large amount of money. You will be even more likely to fudge on your tax forms with big sums of money.

Determine to be scrupulously honest. Doing so may require a constant focus for some time, but eventually you will form new habits.

Entirely Honest

They must not. . .steal, but must show themselves
to be entirely trustworthy and good.
TITUS 2:9–10 NLT

Many people who wouldn't think of stealing even a piece of candy from a corner store feel no compunction against taking materials or supplies from their workplace. Or they make false statements on their tax forms to save hundreds of dollars.

This attitude seems to have particular appeal if life has dealt them some hard or unfair financial blows. They then reason that they are just "evening things up." Take this one step further and they refuse to speak up if a department store undercharges them $50 for an item. They reason that it is the store's job, not theirs, to catch such things. So much for being too honest to steal a piece of candy.

Often, however, people start off being dishonest with small amounts and progress to being dishonest with larger sums. This is why Christians are to be "*entirely* trustworthy and good" (emphasis added)— honest in that which is least and honest in that which is much.

Make up your mind that you are going to be honest no matter what the temptation before you ever face temptation.

Dishonest Gain

*Dishonest money dwindles away, but whoever gathers
money little by little makes it grow.*
PROVERBS 13:11 NIV

What do you do when crooked businesspeople prosper
all around you and never seem to get caught? Meanwhile you work hard, operate honestly, but struggle
to stay afloat, let alone get ahead. You can barely sock
away enough funds to pay your taxes, and you often
dread Christmas because it is a yearly reminder of how
financially tight you are.

Judgment may not come suddenly on the dishonest, but their money often slowly bleeds from their
bank accounts and dwindles away. But if you faithfully
set a little aside—even if it isn't much—over time it
grows.

Remember, however: This is a financial principle, true in most situations over time, not an ironclad
promise that invariably comes to pass.

This fact remains: "Better the little that the righteous have than the wealth of many wicked" (Psalm
37:16 NIV). This is why James says, "Believers who are
poor have something to boast about, for God has honored them" (James 1:9 NLT).

Distrust

Creating Mistrust

Don't plot harm against your neighbor,
for those who live nearby trust you.
PROVERBS 3:29 NLT

Keeping your eyes open so that you aren't taken in by every smooth talker is prudent. But some people don't trust anyone and imagine the worst motives in everyone. Suspicion is often mistaken and unwarranted, and can sometimes be a thinly disguised hatred for others.

On the other hand, don't betray the trust that others have in you. Don't take advantage of family members' generosity. Don't defraud friends who are compassionate. And don't borrow items and neglect to return them.

Don't even destroy others' trust in you by failing to keep your word, by making excuses to back out of commitments, or by being habitually late for appointments. All these things chip away at relationships and create distrust.

How do you do all this? Simple: Love your neighbor. "Love does no harm to a neighbor" (Romans 13:10 NIV). If you distrust and hate your neighbor, you will constantly scheme up ways to make his life more difficult. If you love him, you will be conscious of attitudes and actions that might hurt him, and will avoid these things.

Bitter Disbelief

*Behold, if the LORD would make windows
in heaven, might this thing be?*
2 KINGS 7:2 KJV

There is no denying it: Some people have had difficult lives. They didn't have a privileged upbringing and weren't spared this world's harsh realities. They have had to work hard and have frequently suffered misfortune.

Unfortunately, however, sometimes they become cynical. If others have taken advantage of them or defrauded them, they find it very difficult to trust people. And if they attribute their adversities to God, they conclude that He is not worth trusting either.

One time Samaria was besieged for months and the people suffered famine. When Elisha promised that God would supply abundant food the next day, an official retorted, "If the LORD would make windows in heaven, might this thing be?" He was saying that there was no way this could happen. Even if it looked like it was about to happen, it still wouldn't.

God knows when you have had a tough row to hoe, and He knows a hard life has the potential to make you bitter, but He still asks you to trust Him, to keep your heart tender toward Him through it all.

Suspiciously Critical

We're not in charge of how you live out the faith,
looking over your shoulders, suspiciously critical.
2 CORINTHIANS 1:24 MSG

Paul had founded the church in Corinth, and as their father in the Lord, he wrote them "about the authority the Lord gave us for building you up" (2 Corinthians 10:8 NIV). Elsewhere he explained, "Not that we lord it over your faith, but *we work with you* for your joy" (2 Corinthians 1:24 NIV, emphasis added).

When you are first teaching your son or daughter how to drive, you might have to grab the steering wheel a few times to avert a major accident. But if they are to learn how to drive on their own, you must take your hands off the steering wheel—and keep them off.

If you distrust someone's motives or doubt their ability to live out their Christian faith, you find yourself wanting to impose detailed rules on them to "keep them on the straight and narrow." This, however, is legalism and doesn't help them to mature in Christ.

How much better to take Paul's approach—to build others up in the faith and work *with* them to help them grow.

Divorce/Separation

Rejected and Distressed

*"The LORD will call you back as if you were a wife
deserted and distressed in spirit—a wife who
married young, only to be rejected."*
ISAIAH 54:6 NIV

Divorce causes deep pain. If your marriage has ended, you understand this only too well. The emotional pain of such an experience can be excruciating—particularly if you wanted your marriage to continue but your spouse insisted on a divorce. It only compounds the pain if he or she angrily blamed you for all the "irreconcilable differences."

On your wedding day, you promised to be true, and in return, your loved one promised eternal love and faithfulness to you, and only you. That sacred trust has been broken, and to be rejected afterward in anger and bitterness is devastating.

"The LORD God. . .hates divorce" (Malachi 2:16 NKJV), and He hates it for all the same reasons you do. God feels your pain, and it grieves His heart to see you go through such emotional anguish. Also, He knows that the breakup of a marriage has other far-reaching repercussions, particularly if children are involved.

Your spouse may have rejected you, but God will *never* reject you.

God Still Loves You

The fact is, you have had five husbands,
and the man you now have is not your husband.
JOHN 4:18 NIV

Samaritans held to the law of Moses, and one Samaritan woman took advantage of the fact that she was permitted to divorce and remarry several times. She eventually ended up just living with a man, something the Law didn't sanction.

Most people of her town shunned her, which is why she came to the well alone in the heat of the day. But Jesus, who spoke clearly against divorce, had compassion on her and had a profound spiritual conversation with her. She very likely decided to legally marry her partner after Jesus' visit, but the point is this: If you have been through a divorce and feel condemned, if you feel like an outcast and a failure, if you wonder if God forgives you, remember Jesus' love and beautiful conversation with the Samaritan woman.

He didn't condemn her. Instead, He led her gently to living water and even used her to bring His truth to her town. God still loves you and longs to speak to you as well.

When Love Isn't There

Then she said to him, "How can you say,
'I love you,' when your heart is not with me?"
JUDGES 16:15 NKJV

Sometimes you simply don't feel "in love" anymore. There are things you can do to rejuvenate caring and intimacy, but when you have let things slide for a long time, it takes a complete change of mind and a strong commitment to restore romance. And you may not feel up to it right now.

A temporary separation may be helpful. Paul wrote, "A wife must not separate from her husband. But if she does, she must remain unmarried or else be reconciled to her husband" (1 Corinthians 7:10–11 NIV). At times couples simply need a breather, a little space to think things through.

Often even a separation is unnecessary. When your heart isn't with your spouse anymore, you can't fake the rosy flush of love, but you can show kindness, thoughtfulness, and do small loving acts. And if you are intent on saving your marriage, you will keep at it.

If the other person doesn't respond immediately, don't give up. It can take a while to rekindle emotions of love.

Doubt

Breaking Free from Disbelief

"Why do doubts rise in your minds?"
LUKE 24:38 NIV

Some people seem prone to doubting, trapped in a disbelieving mind-set. Even Jesus' disciples were often this way. After His resurrection, "He rebuked their unbelief and hardness of heart, because they did not believe" (Mark 16:14 NKJV). Some people, like Thomas, seem especially inclined to being skeptical.

If you realize your faith isn't strong and you don't have confidence that God will answer your prayers, you can take steps to increase your faith. First, you must earnestly desire greater faith and, like the disciples, plead, "Increase our faith" (Luke 17:5 NKJV). God will certainly answer such sincere requests, though it may take a while.

When God begins to increase your faith and you see your prayers being answered, then do all you can to encourage it. Paul wrote to Timothy, "Fan into flame the gift of God, which is in you" (2 Timothy 1:6 NIV). God had given Timothy a spiritual gift, and now that this gift was in Timothy's possession, he needed to stir it up, to fan the burning ember into a fire.

Willing Disbelief

But though he had done so many miracles before them,
yet they believed not on him.
JOHN 12:37 KJV

Jesus was often disappointed that His disciples lacked faith. When they feared during a storm, He asked, "Why are you so afraid? Do you still have no faith?" (Mark 4:40 NIV). He asked again, "Where is your faith?" (Luke 8:25 NIV). He expected them to have more faith.

One time Jesus visited His hometown of Nazareth. Mark 6:2 (NIV) says that the people of Nazareth were "amazed" that Jesus exhibited such miraculous powers. For His part, "He was amazed at their lack of faith" (v. 6 NIV). Their faith was so unreasonably, stubbornly small because they were refusing to believe.

But you can choose to have faith. And when you have difficulty believing, you can pray, "Lord, I believe; help my unbelief!" (Mark 9:24 NKJV). The fact is, you *need* faith if you are to truly trust God and survive the storms of life.

No, you can't work up faith by your own efforts, but having the desire to trust God is an excellent place to start. Cry out to God today to increase your faith.

Pleasing or Displeasing God

It's impossible to please God apart from faith.
HEBREWS 11:6 MSG

God loves faith—that is, *real* faith, not constant proclamations of faith when you are actually uncertain. The Bible says that it is impossible to please God if you don't have faith, and to have faith, you must trust Him. To trust Him, you must first come to the realization that God can be trusted.

You may be of a rational mind-set. Believing things without evidence doesn't come easy for you. That's not a problem. God doesn't expect you to jettison your brain and leap naively into the dark. He is willing to prove that He can be trusted (John 2:23; 14:29).

The catch is, once He provides proof He expects you to transfer your trust to Him. But many people are unwilling to do so. "Although He had done so many signs before them, they did not believe in Him" (John 12:37 NKJV).

Jesus was willing to provide compelling evidence to doubting Thomas (John 20:26–28). He will do the same for you if you sincerely seek and ask (Matthew 7:7–8). But you must seek the Lord wholeheartedly, sincerely wanting to know the truth.

Doubts Create Instability

If ye will not believe, surely ye shall not be established.
ISAIAH 7:9 KJV

God has made many clear promises in the Bible. He has promised that if you love and obey Him, He will protect you, He will provide for all your needs, and He will be with you during times of trouble.

You need to do your part, to be sure. But if you do, you can then trust that God will keep His Word and do His part. If, however, you feel that He is either unable or unwilling to do so, you have a breakdown in trust and communication. And as Isaiah said, "If ye will not believe, surely ye shall not be established."

You sometimes can't prevent being assailed by a barrage of doubts. Often the devil hurls "fiery darts" to try to shake you from your position and force you to retreat. At such times, you need to raise your shield of faith to deflect them (Ephesians 6:16 NKJV).

Use the faith you do have "that you may be able to withstand in the evil day, and having done all, to stand" (Ephesians 6:13 NKJV). Do this and you will be established.

Drug Abuse

Hallucinogenic Drugs

Reuben found some mandrakes in the field
and brought them home to his mother Leah.
GENESIS 30:14 MSG

One day Jacob's young son Reuben was wandering through the grain fields when he found an unusual plant: The roots appeared to be a distorted human figure and had a pungent smell (Song of Solomon 7:13). Excited, he took it to his mother, who recognized it as a mandrake. According to local lore, it enhanced fertility.

Mandrakes also contain psychedelic properties and for millennia have been used in superstitious practices and pagan magic rituals. Just because the use of certain hallucinogenic plants is accepted, however, doesn't mean God's people should indulge in them.

Some people argue that God created plants like mandrakes, marijuana, and psychedelic mushrooms, then point out that the Bible says, "God saw everything that He had made, and indeed it was very good" (Genesis 1:31 NKJV). They then contend that God intended people to enjoy eating or smoking them.

But nature has clearly fallen and is now corrupt (Romans 8:21 NKJV). For example, mushrooms such as *Amanita phalloides* (death cap) are deadly poisonous. Clearly, God intends you to have the wisdom to avoid certain plants.

Defiling God's Temple

If anyone defiles the temple of God, God will destroy him.
For the temple of God is holy, which temple you are.
1 CORINTHIANS 3:17 NKJV

At first drugs are an exciting thrill. You never knew you could experience such things—the stresses and boredom of your daily life seem a million miles away. And the fact that they are illegal sometimes makes them seem even more desirable.

But drugs have a harsh long-term effect on your mind and body. The ecstasy you enjoy comes with an excessively high price tag. After a while, you need greater doses to achieve the same pleasurable feelings. Also, you can easily become addicted, with your body craving stimulation whenever you are not high.

If you are a Christian, the Spirit of God lives within you. Your body is His temple. If you willfully defile your body, God removes His protection from you and allows you to suffer the consequences of your actions. God destroys you by allowing you to destroy yourself. In addition, full recovery isn't guaranteed, even if you stop.

Your body is meant to be holy and dedicated to God, so don't vandalize it.

Repenting of Drug Use

*They did not repent of their murders or their sorceries
or their sexual immorality or their thefts.*
REVELATION 9:21 NKJV

The word "sorceries" in the above passage comes from the Greek word *pharmakon*, which refers to drugs. (This is related to our modern word *pharmacy*, a drugstore.) So when the Bible says that people "did not repent of. . .their sorceries," it is saying that they refused to repent of their drug abuse.

When battling a drug addition, people can't change themselves, but God does ask them to repent of it. Repenting is something they can do. They must be ashamed of and hate the sin, they must turn to God and plead for Him to change them, then cooperate with what He does in them.

When the transforming power of God's Spirit enters someone's life, He begins to make changes. If the person has truly turned to God, change will manifest. But she or he must abide in Christ to maintain this victory. "Prove by the way you live that you have repented of your sins and turned to God" (Matthew 3:8 NLT).

This doesn't necessarily mean that victory will come easily, but it will come.

Dysfunctional Relationships

Roots of Sibling Rivalry

*When his brothers realized that their father loved
him more than them, they grew to hate him—
they wouldn't even speak to him.*
GENESIS 37:4 MSG

Jacob loved Joseph more than his other sons because
he was the son of Jacob's beloved wife Rachel. It's
sometimes easy for modern parents as well to favor one
child above another—especially if that child is more
obedient, attractive, or talented. You may do this without even realizing it. "But if you show favoritism, you
sin" (James 2:9 NIV).

While you may not intend to be partial, showing favoritism engenders a sense of entitlement in the
favored child and insecurity in the less-favored child.
And it sets the stage for a lifetime of sibling rivalries.
Many adults trace the roots of dysfunctional family
relationships back to childhood influences.

A parent's approval is vitally important to a child's
emotional and spiritual well-being. It influences their
understanding of God's love and acceptance, views that
persist into adulthood. If you have unwittingly contrib-
uted to sibling rivalries, you can still make amends now
by deliberately, consciously showing love and attention
to all your children equally.

Responding to Bullying

Peninnah would taunt Hannah and make fun of her. . . . Year after year it was the same.
1 SAMUEL 1:6–7 NLT

Long ago when customs were different, a man named Elkanah had two wives, Peninnah and Hannah. Peninnah had several sons, but Hannah was childless. That was hard enough, but to make matters worse, Peninnah continually taunted Hannah about it, making her life miserable. This situation went on for quite some time.

Some bullies aren't fully aware that their words are causing pain, but others know exactly what they are doing and derive pleasure from causing others anguish. They enjoy causing fear by veiled threats. Even if they call themselves believers, their actions are usually motivated by hatred, and they need to repent.

If you are a victim of constant taunting, talk to mature Christians about it. Often, shining light on a bully's behavior is enough to make him or her desist. Even though bullying is common, people are aware these days that harassment and uttering threats are illegal.

If reporting the situation doesn't fully resolve it, entrust your griefs to God. He is able to change things and to bring peace to you.

Opposed by Family Members

*"Those closest to you, your own brothers and cousins,
are working against you."*
JEREMIAH 12:6 MSG

The prophet Jeremiah had a tough time of it. He lamented, "Alas, my mother, that you gave me birth, a man with whom the whole land strives and contends! . . . Everyone curses me" (Jeremiah 15:10 NIV).

Jeremiah expected the nation to reject him, but he may have hoped that at least his family would be loyal to him. Nevertheless, even they turned against him. Jesus experienced the same thing. "Even His brothers did not believe in Him" (John 7:5 NKJV).

If you follow the Lord, you can expect opposition. Jesus warned, "A man's enemies will be the members of his own household" (Matthew 10:36 NIV). At the end of the day, this opposition can leave you very discouraged.

Some families are already very divided, even without faith in Jesus being factored in. Brothers and sisters are at each other's throats; people aren't talking to each other and backstab each other. God can change even dysfunctional families. But in the meantime, be aware that they oppose you, and don't leave yourself open to their attacks.

Dysfunctional Families

Son dishonors father, daughter rises against her mother,
daughter-in-law against her mother-in-law.
MICAH 7:6 NKJV

The prophet Micah described a low point in Israel's history. It was a time of unprecedented greed and corruption, and the morals and the structure of society were collapsing. All the judges accepted bribes, and families and communities were breaking apart. Things had become so bad that Micah advised, "Do not trust in a friend" (7:5), and said that "a man's enemies are the men of his own household" (7:6).

There are many similarities to today, and for the same reasons: Society is undergoing moral collapse. There is a widespread breakdown in families, not only with an unprecedented number of divorces, but with divisions within families.

Some families have so much dysfunction and strife that the situation may seem to be hopeless. But in the midst of all this, God's solution remains the same: "Love your neighbor as yourself" (Matthew 22:39 NLT)—and this includes flesh-and-blood family members.

Some deep-rooted grievances and divisions may take time and effort before they disappear, but God's love and power are able to resolve even them.

Ungovernable Children

His father had never rebuked him by asking,
"Why do you behave as you do?"
1 KINGS 1:6 NIV

David was Israel's greatest king, a man who loved God wholeheartedly, and God blessed and honored him mightily. "David. . .had not failed to keep any of the LORD's commands all the days of his life—except in the case of Uriah the Hittite" (1 Kings 15:5 NIV).

Some critics, however, insist that David was also a failure as a father, since he never asked his son Adonijah, "Why do you behave as you do?" The behavior in question probably refers to Adonijah thinking that, as oldest son, he should receive both the throne and Abishag. So he "put himself forward" (1 Kings 1:5 NIV; 2:15–17).

Whether David failed or not, many parents do fail to discipline their children, leading them to become spoiled. This creates a dysfunctional relationship. Of course, some teens refuse to be rebuked. The Bible specifically addresses this, reminding children to obey their parents (Exodus 20:12).

Parents are to discipline their children, but the Bible also points out that some children choose their own willful ways, despite correction (Deuteronomy 21:18–21).

Elderly Parents

Caring for Parents

*Their first responsibility is to show godliness at home
and repay their parents by taking care of them.*
1 TIMOTHY 5:4 NLT

For most of human history, people took it for granted that when their parents became elderly, they would take their parents into their homes and look after them. This understanding persists in many countries—and Paul says that such practical demonstrations of love should characterize Christians.

It's good that Christians give to missions or the poor, but "their *first* responsibility is to. . .their parents" (emphasis added). Remember Jesus' reproof to the Pharisees: "You say it is all right for people to say to their parents, 'Sorry, I can't help you. For I have vowed to give to God what I would have given to you.' In this way, you let them disregard their needy parents" (Mark 7:11–12 NLT).

This doesn't mean your parents have to live with you—although it may mean that. They could live in a seniors' home and be perfectly happy and content. But the point is, it is your responsibility to see to it that they *are* receiving adequate care and support. And you certainly should visit them regularly.

A Crown of Glory

The silver-haired head is a crown of glory,
if it is found in the way of righteousness.
PROVERBS 16:31 NKJV

These days it is common for seniors to be great-grandparents and to live well into their eighties and nineties. In Bible times, people were told to respect the elderly. Moses commanded, "You shall rise before the gray headed and honor the presence of an old man" (Leviticus 19:32 NKJV).

When your parents grow old and their hair turns white or silver, they gain a distinguished look. And if they have faithfully served God, the Bible says their hair is "a crown of glory." It's as if they have become royalty. You should respect them even more.

However, as elderly parents' memory begins to fail and their advice comes from a past century, it is easy to ignore what they say. The Bible therefore commands people to show respect by performing such acts as rising to their feet when an elderly person enters a room.

You are to show respect to your parents even when you yourself are an adult.

Respecting Elderly Parents

Listen to your father, who gave you life,
and do not despise your mother when she is old.
PROVERBS 23:22 NIV

Respecting your parents is easy when you are a child. They are the authority figures. But when you become a teen, you tend to rebel to establish your own identity. As a young adult, you reengage with them as equals but still respect them, usually because they are in the prime of life and continue to exhibit much wisdom.

But making the transition can be difficult when roles are reversed and your parents depend on you. When they are elderly, many of your parents' decisions seem naive or stubborn, and you must patiently explain to them or override their decisions. Consequently, you may lose a measure of respect for their decision-making ability. This is inevitable, but don't get to the point that you despise them. Solomon wrote, "Listen to your father. . .and do not despise your mother."

Don't merely humor your parents. Truly respect them, even if you must now take the lead in decisions that affect them. Respecting them means honoring them and treating them with dignity.

The Blessing of Old Age

"Men and women of ripe old age will sit in the streets
of Jerusalem, each of them with cane in
hand because of their age."
ZECHARIAH 8:4 NIV

In ancient Israel, living a long life was considered a great blessing. However, today many seniors only count it a blessing if they also experience good health to enjoy their golden years. They look in dismay on becoming weak, being housebound, or even needing a cane or walker.

But these restrictions often come with the territory and are part of God's overall blessing of advanced age. Zechariah declares that a sign of God's blessing on Israel was if men and women of advanced age sat along the streets of Jerusalem, every one of them with a cane in hand.

Why were they sitting along the streets? Because they didn't have the energy to run around. So they sat and talked and minded their grandchildren (Zechariah 8:5). Why did all of them need canes? To help them walk. . .slowly.

Your aged parents' weakness need not detract from the blessing of God in their lives.

Enemies

Beset by Enemies

Consider my enemies, for they are many;
and they hate me with cruel hatred.
PSALM 25:19 NKJV

Things are often difficult enough already, but some-times people set themselves up as your enemies and go out of their way to make your life miserable. Paul warned that people would oppose you simply for being a Christian. "Everyone who wants to live a godly life in Christ Jesus will be persecuted" (2 Timothy 3:12 NIV).

Paul added, "Not that the troubles should come as any surprise to you. . . . It's part of our calling" (1 Thessalonians 3:3 MSG). But to expect troubles is one thing; to experience them on an unrelenting basis is quite another.

David prayed for God to consider his enemies because they were wearing him down, and there were many of them. He had practically wandered into a hornets' nest. It was enough to make him throw up his hands and quit.

David said elsewhere, "I had fainted, unless I had believed to see the goodness of the LORD" (Psalm 27:13 KJV). But he did believe the Lord would be good to him. That is why he prayed for God's help.

Attacks by Enemies

*My enemies would hound me all day, for there are
many who fight against me, O Most High.*
PSALM 56:2 NKJV

David wrote this complaint when he was fleeing from
King Saul and had been arrested by the Philistines.
And after he escaped the Philistines, he was back to
staying ahead of Saul. David's own people, the Israelites, were betraying him to Saul. He certainly had
many fighting against him.

David had done nothing wrong, yet he was on the
run like a fugitive. Do you ever feel that way? You try
to do what's right but only succeed in angering corrupt
people. Instead of being commended for the good you
do, you create jealous enemies. Talk about being mis-
understood! Jesus also had many enemies, through no
fault of His own.

At times in your life you may face strong opposition. Like David, your only hope of surviving
will be to focus your thoughts steadfastly on God
and cry out to Him. Otherwise you will go under,
because nobody can take constant harassment and
persecution.

Thank God for times of peace. But be assured that
He is also with you during times of trouble.

Whispering against You

All my enemies whisper together against me;
they imagine the worst for me.
PSALM 41:7 NIV

Often, your enemies aren't able to do anything to actually hurt you. But that won't stop them from gossiping about you and imagining the worst about you and for you.

When people have decided that you are a bad person, they think all your motives are bad. No matter what you do, they condemn you. You probably wish that such people would get on with their lives and quit trying to wreck yours. But you can't control their attitudes or behavior. You can only control your own.

Ask God to give you peace, and don't worry about them. Keep your heart free of hatred. Jesus said, "Love your enemies, bless them that curse you, do good to them that hate you, and pray for them which despitefully use you, and persecute you" (Matthew 5:44 KJV).

If you love your enemies and ignore the gossip that you hear them saying, "even if they accuse you of doing wrong, they will see your honorable behavior, and they will give honor to God" (1 Peter 2:12 NLT).

God Will Defend You

"You must worship only the LORD your God.
He is the one who will rescue you from all your enemies."
2 KINGS 17:39 NLT

You must spend time in God's presence worshiping Him and acknowledging that He alone is God. It's not that He needs you to remind Him of this fact, however. He is already aware of it. He says, "I am the LORD, and there is none else, there is no God beside me" (Isaiah 45:5 KJV).

But it is important that you know that God is the only one true God as well. This is why God says, "Be still, and know that I am God" (Psalm 46:10 KJV). You need to truly know that He is the all-powerful God. When you know this, you have faith to ask Him to protect you.

If you have enemies who are committed to doing you harm, you need an even more powerful ally who is committed to guarding you from all your enemies. And you have such a friend. When your enemies attack, as they sometimes will, God will rise up to rescue you.

You worship God because He is worthy to be worshiped. But doing so also has powerful benefits.

God Rescues You

You won't be handed over to those men whom you have
good reason to fear. Yes, I'll most certainly save you.
JEREMIAH 39:17 MSG

Baruch came from an influential family of scribes in
Jerusalem, and he served as a scribe for the prophet
Jeremiah, writing down his prophecies. But because he
helped such an unpopular public figure, he had many
powerful enemies.

Baruch was aware that people wanted him dead.
But God promised that no matter what political pressures were at work behind the scenes, he wouldn't
be handed over to them. God would most certainly
defend him.

God has made many, many promises in His Word
to protect His people. If He had said these things just
once or twice, you couldn't be so certain of His inten-
tions. But He has made it abundantly clear that it is
His will to protect you, and He repeatedly tells you
not to fear.

At one point, the Jews complained, "The LORD
has forsaken me, the LORD has forgotten me." But
God replied, "Can a mother forget the baby at her
breast. . . ? Though she may forget, I will not forget
you!" (Isaiah 49:14–15 NIV).

Facing Death

The Land of No Return

*When a few years are come, then I shall go
the way whence I shall not return.*
JOB 16:22 KJV

When you were young, you probably felt you were nearly immortal. Death, when you even thought about it, was very far off. It was easy to joke about it. But as you get older, you take it more seriously. You finally realize that, yes, you will die one day and it will be final.

As a Christian, you know that you will go into the presence of the Lord. So death has lost much of its sting. But the best news is that when Jesus returns, your body will be resurrected in great glory and power. In that sense, you do return. But Job was right: You don't return in your weak mortal body once it dies.

You don't need to fear death. Still, dying is a serious matter, and it is understandable that you will feel sorrow at the thought of leaving loved ones and all that is familiar. And regarding your work, you may regret leaving certain tasks unfinished. So even the thought of going to heaven can be bittersweet.

What Awaits Beyond?

Then Abraham gave up the ghost, and died in a good
old age, an old man, and full of years.
GENESIS 25:8 KJV

In Abraham's day, people had little knowledge of what
awaited after death. They envisioned a vague, shadowy
realm called Sheol where ghosts lived in a dim twilight
of existence—not really living at all. Was Abraham
apprehensive about dying? He might have been.

Yet Abraham was so blessed that the millions of
people who died after him were carried by angels into
"Abraham's bosom" (Luke 16:22 KJV), a paradise full of
light and comfort. Centuries later Moses and Elijah
came from this heavenly place and "appeared in glori-
ous splendor" (Luke 9:30 NIV).

This was even before Jesus died on the cross and
opened the way to the Father's throne in heaven. We
who die now go directly into the presence of Christ.
To be absent from the body is to be present with the
Lord (2 Corinthians 5:8). For Christians, there is no
uncertainty about what awaits after death.

Paul said, "I desire to depart and be with Christ,
which is better by far" (Philippians 1:23 NIV).

Dying Grace

For this God is our God for ever and ever:
he will be our guide even unto death.
PSALM 48:14 KJV

The writer of Psalm 71 was growing older and becoming painfully aware of his frailty and mortality. He implored, "Do not cast me off in the time of old age. . . . When I am old and grayheaded, O God, do not forsake me" (Psalm 71:9, 18 NKJV).

God gives a beautiful response in Isaiah, saying, "Even to your old age and gray hairs I am he, I am he who will sustain you. I have made you and I will carry you" (Isaiah 46:4 NIV). Not only will God be with you when you grow old, but He will be with you right to your dying moment—and beyond! He will literally be your God forever and ever.

He promised, "I will never leave you nor forsake you" (Hebrews 13:5 NKJV). So He is not going to be with you all your life, only to abandon you when you die. The Spirit of Jesus dwells in your heart, and in that day God will claim you as His very own child and take you to heaven.

Carried Away by Angels

*The beggar died, and was carried
by the angels into Abraham's bosom.*
LUKE 16:22 KJV

When they are about to die, some Christians become radiant with joy and expectation, as if already tinged with the glories of heaven. Some even speak of angels gathering in the room, telling them that it is time to go. So they depart this life with great peace, knowing exactly where they are headed.

Other Christians, while they believe in Jesus, face death with a measure of anxiety and even fear. They don't report seeing angels. So are they not going to paradise?

The answer is that not all people are given a glimpse of the magnificent heavenly dimension before departing this life. Nevertheless, angels come to take all believers home. "And he will send out his angels. . .and they will gather his chosen ones" (Matthew 24:31 NLT).

After describing the sure hope of Jesus returning in the rapture to gather believers to Himself, Paul concludes, "Comfort one another with these words" (1 Thessalonians 4:18 KJV). God's promises give great assurance and comfort that we can trust Him to take us to heaven.

Failure

Success or Failure

They refused to trust him.
So he ended their lives in failure.
PSALM 78:32–33 NLT

Worldly people refuse to trust God yet for years may experience "success." However, as their life comes to a close, the glitter of material possessions and accolades fades, leaving them feeling empty. And in the end, they die, taking nothing with them into eternity.

Although the world may have considered them a success, in God's eyes they failed. "For what shall it profit a man, if he shall gain the whole world, and lose his own soul?" (Mark 8:36 KJV).

Even as a Christian, if you focus inordinately on material things and give little priority to spiritual matters, you will end your days in failure. Neglect the Lord and you will experience a sense of futility. You will still be saved but will reach the end of your life having missed much of what the Lord had planned for you.

How much better to make time for reading scripture, praying, and serving God and others, then arrive in heaven to hear Jesus say, "Well done, good and faithful servant. . . . Enter into the joy of your lord" (Matthew 25:21 NKJV).

Feeling Like a Failure

*"I have labored in vain, I have spent my strength
for nothing and in vain."*
ISAIAH 49:4 NKJV

Some people, as they approach the end of their lives, sigh contentedly that they have no regrets. How different it is for others: They have many regrets! They may feel that most of their life was a failure, especially if they squandered years on alcohol or failed in marriage or as a parent. Or if their biggest accomplishment was to hold down a nine-to-five job and they never did anything outstanding, they may feel as if they accomplished little.

Many Christians could certainly do more for the Lord. However, many people are also too hard on themselves. Even after a lifetime of being faithful to God and their family, they lament, "I have labored in vain." But they can also say with the last part of the verse, "Yet surely my just reward is with the LORD, and my work with my God" (Isaiah 49:4 NKJV).

God sees your faithfulness. You may feel like you have failed, but He says, "I have called him. I will bring him, and he will succeed in his mission" (Isaiah 48:15 NIV).

Doomed to Failure

"Why are you disobeying the LORD's command?
This will not succeed!"
NUMBERS 14:41 NIV

Disobeying God guarantees failure, if not immediately, then in due time. When you ignore His laws, you set yourself up for a fall. It's the same if you jump off a building: You will suffer the painful consequences, because the law of gravity always works.

In the same way, you can't violate God's spiritual laws and prosper. They, too, have consequences. After the Israelites refused to go into the Promised Land, God commanded them to wander in the wilderness. *Then* they decided to invade Canaan, but it was too late. God was no longer with them. Moses warned, "This will not succeed!" Sure enough, they suffered a stinging defeat.

Many people live in failure because they refuse to obey God's laws. Even many Christians live defeated lives, spinning their wheels but accomplishing little of lasting value because they are not obeying God.

You can avoid failure by loving God and following His Word. Ask Him to show you what to do every day. Then do it. "Thank God! He gives us victory. . .through our Lord Jesus Christ" (1 Corinthians 15:57 NLT).

Fruit of Your Labor

Strangers will consume your wealth,
and someone else will enjoy the fruit of your labor.
PROVERBS 5:10 NLT

The Bible commands God's people to avoid sexual sin and states one of the penalties for breaking this rule: "Someone else will enjoy the fruit of your labor." Yet some people won't listen and Solomon describes them later lamenting, "If only I had not ignored all the warnings! . . . I have come to the brink of utter ruin" (Proverbs 5:12, 14 NLT).

People also crash and burn through reckless or dishonest financial practices. If they break those rules, many months or years of hard work can come crashing down. Failing simply because things didn't turn out as you'd hoped after doing your best is one thing. Setting yourself up for failure by cheating or cutting corners is quite another.

God wants to spare you from failure in *every* area of life. His desire is to see you rewarded for all your years of hard work. He wants to see you, not some stranger, enjoy the fruit of your labor. So stay close to Him and obey Him, and you will achieve success.

Family Feuds

Resolving Divisions

They had such a sharp disagreement
that they parted company.
ACTS 15:39 NIV

Paul was the inspired apostle who wrote 1 Corinthians 13, the beautiful "love chapter." For his part, Barnabas "was a good man, full of the Holy Spirit" (Acts 11:24 NKJV), constantly encouraging others (v. 23). You would think that they would get along. And for years they did. But one day they had such a heated argument that they could no longer work together.

It began when they were heading out on their second missionary trip. Barnabas wanted to take his cousin Mark, but Paul was set against it since Mark had deserted them previously. Both men were filled with God's Spirit, but they were also strong-willed and opinionated.

Similar scenarios often replay in today's churches and Christian families. Minor disagreements harden into ill will, with both sides unwilling to humble themselves and take the necessary steps to make amends. This can develop into a major family feud.

However, nursing hard feelings isn't God's way. He longs for love, peace, and reconciliation. Fortunately, Paul, Barnabas, and Mark forgave one another and later worked together again (1 Corinthians 9:6; Colossians 4:10).

Blended Families

"You are not going to get any inheritance in our family,"
they said, "because you are the son of another woman."
JUDGES 11:2 NIV

Jephthah's half brothers rejected him because his
mother was a prostitute with whom their father had
slept. As long as their father was alive, they were
obliged to tolerate Jephthah. But as soon as their father
died, the brothers kicked Jephthah out of the house,
informing him that they had never accepted him as
family.

That had to hurt. While such heavy-handed violence is thankfully rare, this kind of rejection is not
uncommon. Thank God for blended families who live
in harmony, but at times stepsiblings have difficulty
accepting one another. Often this is because parents
show favoritism to their natural children and the stepsiblings resent this. Even biological brothers and sisters
quarrel and fight, but they may be more inclined to
make amends with one another.

If you have God's love in your heart, He will
help you overcome such divisions and differences.
His Word says, "Sympathize with each other. Love
each other as brothers and sisters. Be tenderhearted"
(1 Peter 3:8 NLT).

Sibling Rivalry

*David's oldest brother. . .burned with anger at
him. . . . "Now what have I done?" said David.*
1 SAMUEL 17:28–29 NIV

Eliab, Jesse's oldest son, had a commanding presence
(1 Samuel 16:6–7). He was aware of his good looks
and, as the eldest, demanded respect. But God had
bypassed Eliab and his brothers to pick David, the
youngest. Sibling rivalry was definitely in play.

Jesse had sent David to the battle lines, but Eliab
didn't know that, so he angrily asked, "Why have you
come down here? . . . I know how conceited you are
and how wicked your heart is; you came down only
to watch the battle" (1 Samuel 17:28 NIV). "Now what
have I done?" David asked. He was apparently used to
Eliab verbally attacking him.

You may have a sharp-tongued brother or sister
who is quick to misjudge you and is constantly ascrib-
ing wrong motives to you. Your sibling may be jealous,
or perhaps you had a run-in years earlier and he or she
has never gotten over it.

Whatever your sibling may do, refuse to answer tit
for tat. Rise above sibling rivalry, be at peace with your
family, and seek to restore broken relationships.

Avoid Troublemakers

Here are six things GOD
hates. . .a troublemaker in the family.
PROVERBS 6:16, 19 MSG

Some people have a permanent negative attitude and try to make others miserable with their constant criticism, quickness to take offense, and continual complaining. Or they spread gossip, creating animosity and suspicion. Perhaps there is someone like that in your extended family.

In Proverbs 6, Solomon lists six things God particularly dislikes, and number six is "a troublemaker in the family." The New Living Translation has "a person who sows discord in a family." The New International Version has "a person who stirs up conflict." So having a troublemaker in the family was a common problem even back then.

Proverbs 22:10 (NKJV) says, "Cast out the scoffer, and contention will leave; yes, strife. . .will cease." You can't cast an unpleasant person out of the family, but the takeaway here is that you can avoid spending time in that person's company.

If you must invite a family troublemaker to a get-together, be aware of where she is at, and don't take her comments to heart. Let her negativity roll like water off a duck's back. And pray that God will either change her or limit the damage she does.

Family Stress

Doing Your Fair Share

*"Lord, do You not care that my sister has left me
to serve alone? Therefore tell her to help me."*
LUKE 10:40 NKJV

Martha was "worried and troubled about many things"
(Luke 10:41 NKJV). Jesus, Israel's Messiah, was visiting,
and she wanted to present a splendid feast. They were
likely a wealthy family and may have had servants. If
so, Martha could have left the cooking and serving to
them, but she insisted on micromanaging preparations.

Her sister, Mary, however, had chosen to listen to
Jesus. After all, Israel's Messiah was visiting, and she
wanted to make the most of the opportunity. Jesus
commended Mary and refused to send her into the
kitchen.

Most modern homes don't have servants, so the
right thing to do is to get up and help do the work
that needs to be done. If not, one person ends up doing
it all—whether cleaning, cooking, dishes, or whatever.
And if this becomes a regular pattern, it creates stress
in the home.

In a family, every member needs to pull his or her
share of the load. Even children should have regular
duties and fulfill them.

Feeling Unappreciated

*"You have made them equal to us who have
borne the burden of the work."*
MATTHEW 20:12 NIV

When the prodigal son staggered home, filthy and starving, his father threw a feast. His other son complained, "I've stayed here serving you, never giving you one moment of grief, but have you ever thrown a party for me and my friends? Then this son of yours. . .shows up and you go all out with a feast!" (Luke 15:29–30 MSG). It didn't seem fair.

Because the older brother had worked hard every day and tried his best to please his father, he felt unappreciated when his father threw a party for his prodigal brother. Actually, the father was simply celebrating seeing a son whom he had feared dead. Likewise, modern children sometimes misread their parents' motives.

When one of your children is struggling, you may show them extra attention, but although your motives are good, be aware of how things might look to your other children, and explain that you deeply appreciate them and all they do.

"We are taking pains to do what is right, not only in the eyes of the Lord but also in the eyes of man" (2 Corinthians 8:21 NIV).

Caring for Your Family

Anyone who neglects to care for family members
in need repudiates the faith.
1 TIMOTHY 5:8 MSG

The Bible says that a strong proof that your faith is genuine is if you love other Christians (John 13:35). It also says that even if you say you love God, you are lying if you hate other believers (1 John 4:20). And you are expected to prove your love in practical ways by sharing food and clothing with them if they are in need (1 John 3:16–18).

It should come as no surprise therefore that God considers love for your immediate family to be definitive proof of your faith. And He expects you to demonstrate love by caring, tangible actions.

Your primary duty as mothers and fathers is to provide food, clothing, and shelter for your children, to meet their medical and dental needs, and to spend time with them, nurturing them. If you are divorced, be faithful with child support. Don't look on it as a burden, but provide cheerfully.

Much needless stress is caused when parents fail to grasp the importance of these basic responsibilities. But obeying this principle is obeying the heart of Jesus' message.

Meeting Expectations

Fathers, do not exasperate your children;
instead, bring them up in the training
and instruction of the Lord.
EPHESIANS 6:4 NIV

Paul instructed fathers not to exasperate their children. Most parents, however, feel that their children's behavior is more likely to exasperate them. You try to train them to do the right things, but they often stubbornly resist, complain, fight with their brothers and sisters, and make you unhappy. This creates ongoing stress in the home and is liable to produce short tempers.

Here is where you have to have faith that a loving approach, constant instruction, and consistent training will eventually have an effect, transform your children from the inside out, and round off their rough edges.

If you lose faith in the gentle approach, you may try sledgehammer tactics, barking out commands and forcing your child to obey. That may well produce immediate outward results, but it won't work in the long run. And it will exasperate your children.

How much better to involve your child in the process! It may take longer for their behavior to change and for them to meet your expectations, but the change will be genuine and lasting.

Fragmented Families

All the others care only for themselves
and not for what matters to Jesus Christ.
PHILIPPIANS 2:21 NLT

For thousands of years, one of the defining traits of a family was that individual members cared for each other, pulled together, and did their share to make things work. The following verse about the church also holds true for a healthy family: "There should be no schism. . .members should have the same care for one another" (1 Corinthians 12:25 NKJV).

Unfortunately, this is not the case in many modern families. Many families are divided and fragmented. Often parents and brothers and sisters live in the same house but "care only for themselves."

Christians proclaim their love and faith in God, but if they focus on what matters to Jesus, they realize the importance of loving their fellow humans, beginning with their own family members. "He has given us this command: Anyone who loves God must also love their brother and sister" (1 John 4:21 NIV).

Yes, people these days are busy, and they have their own interests. This is understandable. But they need to interact in love and help one another as a family.

Fear

I Shall Not Fear

Whenever I am afraid, I will trust in You.
PSALM 56:3 NKJV

King David had many enemies and was constantly fighting battles against them. He admitted that he felt fear at times, but he had also learned from experience what to do in such situations. Rather than give in to his fear and run, he cried out to the Lord.

David said to God, "Whenever I am afraid, I will trust in You" (Psalm 56:3 NKJV). You notice that David didn't say, "*If* I am afraid"—as if he was so brave that it was highly unlikely he would experience fear. He said, "*Whenever* I am afraid." He, too, knew fear. But he knew how to deal with it: He trusted God.

Trusting in God means you believe that God will protect you. This is why David also said, "Though I walk through the valley of the shadow of death, I will fear no evil; for You are with me" (Psalm 23:4 NKJV). Fear is a very common human emotion, and that is why the Bible has so much to say about it and tells us so often how to overcome it.

Unshaken by Bad News

*They do not fear bad news; they confidently trust
the LORD to care for them.*
PSALM 112:7 NLT

Psalm 112 opens by saying, "How joyful are those who
fear the LORD and delight in obeying his commands"
(v. 1 NLT). These are the people whom verse 7 (NLT)
refers to, saying, "They do not fear bad news; they confidently trust the LORD to care for them."

King Ahaz, however, is an example of someone who didn't love or trust God. When he heard
news that his two worst enemies were conspiring to
invade his land, "the hearts of Ahaz and his people
were shaken, as the trees of the forest are shaken by
the wind" (Isaiah 7:2 NIV).

If you are constantly in the habit of looking to
God, it is much easier for you to trust Him when trouble comes. For one thing, if you know you are doing
your best to obey Him, you have more assurance that
He will answer your prayers. "God does not hear sinners; but if anyone is a worshiper of God and does His
will, He hears him" (John 9:31 NKJV).

Confidently trust in God. He is looking out for you.

Overcoming Fear

"You will live in such fear that the sound of a leaf
driven by the wind will send you fleeing."
LEVITICUS 26:36 NLT

God warned that if His people disobeyed Him, "I will make their hearts so fearful. . .that the sound of a wind-blown leaf will put them to flight. They will run. . .and they will fall, even though no one is pursuing them" (Leviticus 26:36 NIV). Today we call this paranoia.

God doesn't desire His children to live in fear, but people bring fear on themselves through disobedience. "God hath not given us the spirit of fear; but of power, and of love, and of a sound mind" (2 Timothy 1:7 KJV).

When you depart from God, your protection vanishes and your fears begin to close in on you. Soon you complain, "The thing which I greatly feared is come upon me" (Job 3:25 KJV). Then you are running from your own shadow—or a scuttling leaf.

If you are plagued by fear, repent of any sin in your heart. Then trust God to forgive you, and He will. He promised in His Word that He would (1 John 1:8–9).

Be of Good Courage

Be strong and of a good courage, fear not, nor be afraid
of them: for the LORD . . .will not fail thee,
nor forsake thee.
DEUTERONOMY 31:6 KJV

Fear is a tremendously debilitating thing. It can suck the life right out of you. It can make you throw up your hands in defeat before the fight even begins. And if you were in this by yourself, that might be a logical thing to do. After all, why face an enemy who vastly outguns you?

But there is a good reason to have courage: The Lord is on your side. He won't cave in when you need Him most; He won't suddenly realize that He is not strong enough; nor will He abandon you in your crisis. These are very encouraging thoughts.

The enemy will try to overwhelm you with feelings of apprehension, but remind yourself of who is on your side and face down your fear. Don't blink, and even if you are hit with a wave of fear, stand your ground. That wave is merely a tactic of the enemy and will crash harmlessly against the great Rock on which you have taken refuge.

Financial Strain

Waiting for Economic Recovery

"All this misery is from the LORD!
Why should I wait for the LORD any longer?"
2 KINGS 6:33 NLT

In the days of King Jehoram of Israel, the Syrians had besieged Samaria, and the siege lasted so long that there was a great famine: A donkey's head was sold for eighty shekels ($1,120), and one cup of dove's dung sold for five shekels ($70) (2 Kings 6:25 KJV).

Elisha had been advising the king to trust God, but finally the king snapped, stormed up to Elisha's door, and shouted, "All this misery is from the LORD! Why should I wait for the LORD any longer?"

Your faith can be tested to the limit when you wait and wait for a financial breakthrough, to the point where you are tempted to abandon hope. You may conclude that God is against you and is, in fact, the one causing your problems. So you lash out at those who encourage you to hope. Yet in the Israelites' case, the next day God did a miracle and provided enough food for everyone (see 2 Kings 7:1–16).

God can still do miracles today. Don't abandon hope.

Soaring Food Costs

*A loaf of wheat bread or three loaves
of barley will cost a day's pay.*
REVELATION 6:6 NLT

During times of war, natural disaster, or drought, the price of food has always risen—and the Bible warns that during the closing chapter of earth's history, prices will rise to astronomical levels.

Food prices have already increased dramatically in recent years. One of the main reasons is that farm machinery consumes much fuel, as do the trucks that transport food. Also, major aquifers that farmers have depended on for decades are running dry. In addition, year after year of no rainfall in major food-producing regions is causing prices to spike.

All of these factors have put a constant financial strain on families, who must now allocate a greater portion of their monthly budget to food.

The short-term solution is to find ways to earn a little extra cash, learn to budget better, and do without nonessentials. But the only solution to the final tribulation and food crisis is for God to bring paradise down to earth, creating justice and plenty for all. As Christians, we earnestly wait for that day.

Uncertain Finances

Take no thought for your life,
what ye shall eat, or what ye shall drink.
MATTHEW 6:25 KJV

Many Christians consider the phrase "Take no thought for your life" to be impractical advice. How can you help but take constant thought for your life? You need to stay on top of every detail of your work and home life to make sure things get done.

But a more accurate translation is, "Take no *anxious thought* for your life." This is why both the NIV and the NKJV translate this phrase, "Do not worry about your life."

You may have a steady nine-to-five job that holds no surprises and supplies a guaranteed paycheck. Although you find your work somewhat boring, you don't worry much. But Christ's admonition is especially comforting when you run your own business, are self-employed, or work on commission, and your finances alternate between feast and famine.

And in difficult financial times, with employment more insecure and steadily rising prices, you need the reassurance that God will supply all your needs. He has promised to do just that (see Philippians 4:19). So don't worry.

Running Up Debt

It's stupid to try to get something for nothing,
or run up huge bills you can never pay.
PROVERBS 17:18 MSG

Contrary to the Bible's warnings, many Christians hope to benefit from monetary windfalls without doing any work. They daydream of winning the lottery and enjoying a life of ease.

It's just as irresponsible to constantly pull out their credit card and run up huge bills with no idea how they will be able to repay them. They may be hoping that God will bless them with huge finances out of left field, but that is not the way God made His world to work.

God's basic financial plan hasn't changed in thousands of years: "Whoever gathers money little by little makes it grow," and "hard work brings a profit, but mere talk leads only to poverty" (Proverbs 13:11; 14:23 NIV).

Of course, when starting up a new business, you often must borrow money to launch out. There are times when you need to take calculated financial risks—with the emphasis on "calculated." You should have a well-thought-out plan on how you will repay the money. Do that and you will avoid much financial stress.

Giving Wisely

I do not mean that others should be eased
and you burdened.
2 CORINTHIANS 8:13 NKJV

When Paul was writing to the Corinthians about giving money to help the impoverished Christians in Jerusalem, he assured them that God would bless them for giving generously but didn't want them donating so much that they themselves ended up financially short.

You are required to give to God, and many Christians believe in tithing 10 percent of their income. But some churches also encourage people to give "freewill offerings" above and beyond that. A few, quoting Mark 12:41–44, pressure you to "sacrificially" give money you have allocated for food and rent. This can leave you under intense financial strain.

If you can afford to give and feel you should, by all means do. But avoid being pressured to give if you don't have it to spare. You may be asked to donate to a truly worthy cause, but your first responsibility is to care for your family.

God blesses generous giving, but He also gives you wisdom to help you avoid spending money you shouldn't spend or giving money you shouldn't give and thereby bringing hardship on yourself.

Foreclosure/Eviction

Losing Your Home

*Even now we go hungry
and thirsty. . .and have no home.*
1 Corinthians 4:11 nlt

It's devastating to be uprooted and lose your home. But if you can no longer afford to pay your mortgage, you have no choice but to give up your house. Then you are often forced to move from one cheap rental to another.

Jesus didn't have a home, either. After His life's work began, He was constantly on the road. He said, "Foxes have dens to live in, and birds have nests, but the Son of Man has no place even to lay his head" (Matthew 8:20 nlt). He gave up His home to travel around sharing the Gospel.

Paul didn't have a home, either. He had "no certain dwellingplace" (1 Corinthians 4:11 kjv). He was constantly moving from place to place, never sure where he would sleep next. But he accepted this and said, "If we have food and clothing, we will be content with that" (1 Timothy 6:8 niv).

If you are discouraged over losing your house, remember: This world is not your promised home. God is preparing a mansion in heaven for you.

Driven from Home

They were forced to live in the dry stream beds,
among the rocks and in holes in the ground.
JOB 30:6 NIV

Bible lands often had a turbulent history, with invading armies sweeping across the landscape or civil wars causing upheavals. People were forced from their homes and took shelter wherever they could. "They wandered in the wilderness. . .they found no city to dwell in" (Psalm 107:4 KJV).

This scenario is being repeated in war-torn nations today. Christians in countries like Syria and Iraq have had to flee their homes on short notice or be executed.

We can be thankful for the peace we enjoy. Still, these are troubled times, and many people in our nation are forced out of their homes through foreclosure. Being uprooted from your home of many years can be a traumatic experience.

Even though you know that some people have troubles much worse than yours, that doesn't invalidate your suffering. God sympathizes with your pain, too. And your sorrow gives you greater empathy for the suffering of others. It also gives you good reason to be thankful when you find a secure place once again.

Thrust from the Nest

The women of Moab are left like homeless birds.
ISAIAH 16:2 NLT

In Isaiah's day, the Assyrians were invading Judah—as well as Moab to the east. Isaiah described a situation where the men of Moab had been defeated in battle and the women and children were fleeing their towns ahead of the advancing armies.

The New International Version describes them "like fluttering birds pushed from the nest" (Isaiah 16:2 NIV). If you have ever seen a baby bird fluttering frantically and helplessly, you get an idea of the panic and loss these women were experiencing.

Perhaps you can identify. You can if you are being evicted from your home—either because you can no longer pay your mortgage or are behind on your rent. Not knowing where you will move to can be overwhelming. Like Abraham, you head out, not knowing where you are going (Hebrews 11:8).

But God promised the wandering Israelites, "I am sending an angel ahead of you to guard you along the way and to bring you to the place I have prepared" (Exodus 23:20 NIV). May this promise be a comfort to you as well.

Greed

Greed Destroys Relationships

A greedy and grasping person destroys community.
PROVERBS 15:27 MSG

Greed is a spiritual cancer. It mars and destroys an otherwise beautiful life. It corrupts every relationship it touches. Greed ruins good people, causing them to do deceitful, selfish, and illegal things for unjust gain. And it holds them back from helping the needy.

Greed is the epitome of self-centered living, the exact opposite of what the Gospel teaches. This is why Paul warned, "For of this you can be sure: No immoral, impure or greedy person—such a person is an idolater—has any inheritance in the kingdom of Christ and of God" (Ephesians 5:5 NIV).

Jesus said, "Be on your guard against all kinds of greed; life does not consist in an abundance of possessions" (Luke 12:15 NIV). *True* life consists of loving God and your fellow man. It consists of helping those in desperate situations. It means being an integral part of a caring, sharing family and community.

How do you avoid the cancer of greed? By sincerely loving God and loving your fellow man. Then you won't attempt to gain security and contentment by clutching material things.

Victims of the Greedy

Such is the fate of all who are greedy for money;
it robs them of life.
PROVERBS 1:19 NLT

Have you been a victim of others' greed? Has a salesman led you into paying thousands more for a car than you should have? Have you gone to a store to buy an inexpensive computer but shelled out hundreds more because a sales rep persuaded you to buy programs you didn't even need?

Has someone ever paid you a pittance for collectibles they recognized as valuable? "The shopper says, 'That's junk—I'll take it off your hands,' then goes off boasting of the bargain" (Proverbs 20:14 MSG). Even though the buyer's actions were legal and technically it was up to you to know better, you still feel robbed.

But greedy people are the greatest losers. They may deprive you of money, but greed robs them of life. People only spend a few, short years on earth, then step into eternity, where they reap the eternal rewards of their actions.

So, "knowing that you have a better and an enduring possession for yourselves in heaven" (Hebrews 10:34 NKJV), don't grieve the loss of a few material goods.

Snared by Material Things

"Beware! Guard against every kind of greed.
Life is not measured by how much you own."
LUKE 12:15 NLT

You have heard the empty boast, "He who dies with the most toys, wins." But the fact is, he who dies, *dies*, and someone else gets all his toys. Solomon said, "I must leave it to the man who will come after me" (Ecclesiastes 2:18 NKJV). And Paul noted, "We brought nothing into this world, and it is certain we can carry nothing out" (1 Timothy 6:7 NKJV).

Even while you are alive, life isn't measured by how much you own. Yet many people confidently argue that if you are godly, the Lord will bless you with great wealth. This philosophy seems to be true as long as things are going fine—but it immediately collapses when trouble comes.

"Those who want to get rich fall into temptation and a trap and into many foolish and harmful desires that plunge people into ruin and destruction" (1 Timothy 6:9 NIV). You may be weary of struggling from paycheck to paycheck and living in desperate situations, but being ensnared by material things can be worse still.

Greed Is Idolatry

Put to death, therefore. . .impurity, lust,
evil desires and greed, which is idolatry.
COLOSSIANS 3:5 NIV

The Bible clearly warns that greed is idolatry. Or, as the King James Version says, "covetousness. . .is idolatry." To covet something is to have your heart fully set on something and to focus all your efforts on getting it for yourself. When you are coveting physical things for selfish pleasure, that is greed.

Putting things before your relationship with the Lord is also a form of idol worship. "God. . .gives us richly all things to enjoy" (1 Timothy 6:17 NKJV), but greed desires still more. That is why Paul says that you must wage an aggressive war against greed. You must recognize that it is as bad as lust and evil desires and seek to put it to death.

Of course, you can covet good things instead. The apostle Paul, after a lengthy discussion of the gifts of the Spirit, advises Christians, "Covet earnestly the best gifts" (1 Corinthians 12:31 KJV). You are not only to covet good things, but you are to covet them *earnestly*. Speaking of which, Paul then describes love, the most desirable virtue of all.

Helplessness

You Are Not Helpless

*I can do everything through Christ,
who gives me strength.*
PHILIPPIANS 4:13 NLT

At times you will be overwhelmed by problems and circumstances, and it can be frightening to be swept along by situations that seem to be completely beyond your control.

But although you are powerless to deal with insurmountable problems, you are never completely helpless, because the all-powerful God is with you. Christ lives in you, and He can strengthen you and give you solutions and just the right answers.

The armies of Israel felt helpless against Goliath, but David, emboldened by the Spirit of God, faced the giant and defeated him. Paul tells us, "Be strong in the Lord, and in the power of his might" (Ephesians 6:10 KJV).

Do you feel weak and helpless? Rejoice! This gives God the opportunity to work miracles through you. As Paul wrote, "When I am weak, then am I strong" (2 Corinthians 12:10 KJV). God assured him, "My strength is made perfect in weakness" (12:9 KJV).

Even when things are darkest, you can always pray. God can do the impossible, and with Him on your side, things are never completely out of control.

The Hopes of the Helpless

LORD, you know the hopes of the helpless.
Surely you will hear their cries and comfort them.
PSALM 10:17 NLT

Many people today are helpless. They are boxed into
desperate situations over which they have no control.
Their only recourse is to cry out to God.

This applies to families trying to make ends meet
on a limited budget—only to be hit by a large, unexpected expense. It applies to single mothers trying to
raise children in a difficult part of town. It applies to
seniors struggling with health issues. God knows each
of their sorrows and needs, and He hears their cries
for help.

Usually, however, God doesn't do outstanding miracles and completely transform their situations. Instead,
He answers incrementally, day by day, in almost imper-
ceptible ways, helping them manage through desperate
times and comforting them in their sorrow. "Blessed
be God. . .the Father of mercies, and the God of all
comfort" (2 Corinthians 1:3 KJV).

God knows the hopes of the helpless, His heart is
moved by their pain, and He acts to bring them relief,
even when it seems that He is not present.

Utterly Helpless

I am utterly helpless, without any chance of success.
JOB 6:13 NLT

After losing all his earthly belongings—and even his family—in a series of calamities, and after months of suffering painful boils all over his body, Job was ready to call it quits. He lamented, "I have nothing to live for" (Job 6:11 NLT). He had been completely beaten down.

Job was convinced that no matter what he attempted, he would fail. He had absolutely zero chance of succeeding in anything he tried to do. So why even bother?

Sometimes you may feel that way. Life has dealt you hard blows, and just when you are struggling to get back on your feet, you are knocked down again. It seems as if God has conspired against you, or even if He hasn't, He still isn't with you while life puts you through the wringer.

But God was always there with Job and had never abandoned him—even if it looked as if He had. God just had to take Job through a particularly difficult season of life, and once that was over, He restored Job's riches and caused him to succeed again. He will do the same for you.

God Sees the Helpless

The LORD replies,
"I have seen violence done to the helpless."
PSALM 12:5 NLT

Sometimes you wonder if God actually sees how the wicked oppress the helpless—and if He sees, if He cares—because the wicked keep on hurting the weak. But in the verse above (NLT), God goes on to say, "Now I will rise up to rescue them, as they have longed for me to do."

You may be suffering oppression from someone who has great power, and there is nobody to deliver you out of that person's hand. You may wonder how long it will take for the Lord to act.

God often takes His time, but His delays don't mean that He overlooks the wrong that was done, or *is* being done. He doesn't. And though you may be unable to alter the outcome, God is far from helpless. He is all-powerful, and what is more, He is a just God and cares for you. So He will act.

But He doesn't settle every score and right every wrong in this life. Many He reserves for the day of judgment when the righteous will be rewarded and the unjust will be condemned (2 Thessalonians 1:4–10; James 5:1–9).

Weakness Transformed

Their weakness was turned to strength.
They became strong in battle and put
whole armies to flight.
HEBREWS 11:34 NLT

Hebrews 11:32 mentions Gideon as one of the heroes who accomplished great things. But Gideon started off weak. He protested to the Angel of the Lord, "How can I rescue Israel? My clan is the weakest in the whole tribe of Manasseh, and I am the least in my entire family!" (Judges 6:15 NLT).

Nevertheless, Gideon believed God and gathered an army to fight the Midianites and Amalekites. And because he believed, God made him strong in battle and he put the invading armies to flight.

God often chooses weak, helpless people to accomplish His purposes. He could choose strong people—and sometimes does—but then they tend to get the idea that they were victorious *because* they were strong. But if they know they are weak, they realize they overcame only because God helped them.

You may feel weak and incapable, completely overwhelmed by your circumstances. But if you pray desperately, God can transform your weakness into strength and empower you to do amazing things.

Hidden Sin

God Searches Your Heart

Search me, O God, and know my heart: try me,
and know my thoughts: and see if there
be any wicked way in me.
PSALM 139:23–24 KJV

All Christians sin from time to time. But God is more than willing to forgive. "If we say that we have no sin, we deceive ourselves. . . . If we confess our sins, he is faithful and just to forgive us our sins, and to cleanse us from all unrighteousness" (1 John 1:8–9 KJV).

However, the problem comes when believers don't seek to make things right. Sometimes you don't recognize that you have done wrong, or—as is often the case—you are aware that you have sinned but aren't ready to repent. Or you don't take your sin seriously. You tell yourself that you are only human, and it is a trifling matter, after all.

But sin causes a disconnect in your relationship with God, so it is wise to pray, "Search me, O God," then listen carefully to what He brings to your attention. If you want to walk in the light, you must continually surrender any darkness in your life to God.

Covering Sin

He who covers his sins will not prosper,
but whoever confesses and forsakes them will have mercy.
PROVERBS 28:13 NKJV

Sometimes believers struggle with hidden sin. They are in agony over something they have done but are scared to bring it to the light. The reason is shame or fear: They worry about their reputations. What would people think if they knew they had done such a selfish thing? No, they reason, better to keep it covered. So they continue to suffer—and to miss out on the blessings God longs to give them—because "he who covers his sins will not prosper."

There is wisdom in not describing a private sin (something that concerns only the sinner and God) publicly. Since so many people love gossip, the sinner would only open himself to needless pain. Also, if he has offended someone, the Bible says that the ideal solution is to go to that person alone and apologize (Matthew 18:15).

Confessing certain personal faults to mature spiritual friends is also appropriate at times. "Confess your faults one to another, and pray one for another, that ye may be healed" (James 5:16 KJV). God longs to give you both wisdom and peace.

Addicted to Pornography

They let themselves go in sexual obsession,
addicted to every sort of perversion.
EPHESIANS 4:19 MSG

For believers addicted to pornography, their life alternates between rushes of sexual excitement and condemnation. They know they shouldn't lust over sexual images, but when tempted, they frequently succumb. Over time they let themselves go and no longer exercise any restraint. They know it is wrong but enjoy it so much that they no longer make an effort to stop.

But God is faithful. He never gave up on the prodigal son, even when he was carousing with harlots, and He will never give up on believers today either. He will continue to convict them to bring them to repentance.

Once they determine to obey God, there are effective steps they can take to break free. First, they must ditch any pornographic magazines and block any explicit websites they have been visiting so they can't go back.

Then they must pray every day for the Lord to cleanse their hearts and minds, and to renew their thought patterns.

Achan's Stolen Treasure

"I coveted them and took them.
They are hidden in the ground inside my tent."
JOSHUA 7:21 NIV

An Israelite named Achan disobeyed God's command not to take any of Jericho's treasure, and buried choice items inside his tent. Consequently, God judged the entire nation, causing Israel to suffer their first defeat in battle.

So often the innocent suffer because of the guilty. And like Achan, the guilty cover up what they have done and never confess it. Perhaps you work for a business where items have gone missing and everyone is under suspicion and being penalized for one person's actions.

Or perhaps you were careless or negligent, and because you didn't own up to it right away when the situation still could have been salvaged, you caused your company a major loss. It's an awful feeling to be on the outs with everyone over something you now would have done differently.

The best thing you can do is learn from your lesson and make sure never to repeat it. "He will speak peace to His people. . .but let them not turn back to folly" (Psalm 85:8 NKJV).

Hopelessness

God Never Disregards You

Why do you complain, Jacob? Why do you say,
Israel, "My way is hidden from the LORD;
my cause is disregarded by my God"?
ISAIAH 40:27 NIV

Hope, along with love and faith, is a key virtue (1 Corinthians 13:13). To lose hope leaves a great gnawing emptiness inside you. Though you still believe in God, if you lose hope that He loves you and think that He has turned His face away, you are basically just a shell of yourself.

Imagine being convinced that God cares so little about you that He completely ignores you. He is aware that you are mired in problems, but He simply can't be bothered to help you or comfort you. Talk about hopelessness!

The truth is very different. God loves you, and your cause is constantly before His eyes. He made certain of that by permanently etching your name on His hands. He says, "Can a mother forget the baby at her breast. . . ? Though she may forget, I will not forget you! See, I have engraved you on the palms of my hands" (Isaiah 49:15–16 NIV).

God sees what you are going through, and He cares immensely.

Withstanding Fear

We're all afraid. Everyone in the country feels hopeless.
JOSHUA 2:9 MSG

When God was ready to lead the Israelites into Canaan, He struck great fear into the hearts of the Canaanites so they'd melt away before His people. The Lord did amazing miracles to convince them that it was futile to fight Him. And it worked. The harlot Rahab told the spies, "We're all afraid. Everyone in the country feels hopeless."

However, sometimes God's people experience paralyzing fear, too. This often happens when they are disobeying Him in some way. God warned, "There were they in great fear, where no fear was" (Psalm 53:5 KJV). Many people today are afraid even when they are not in imminent danger. The solution is to get their hearts right with God as quickly as possible. Then the fears and delusions will melt away.

Or the problem might not be sin; perhaps they succumb to fear and think their situation is hopeless because they are not spending enough time in prayer, looking to God. Remember that He promises, "You will keep him in perfect peace, whose mind is stayed on You, because he trusts in You" (Isaiah 26:3 NKJV).

Hopelessly Confused

Live no longer as the Gentiles do,
for they are hopelessly confused.
EPHESIANS 4:17 NLT

Before you were saved, "you were separate from Christ. . .without hope and without God in the world" (Ephesians 2:12 NIV). You were lost and condemned. You had no purpose for living. The Bible describes this, saying: "Our days on earth are like a shadow, without hope" (1 Chronicles 29:15 NIV).

But when Jesus saved you, you gained "hope as an anchor for the soul, firm and secure" (Hebrews 6:19 NIV). This renewed your way of thinking and gave you tremendous peace and joy.

But it is important to grow in your faith and to continue to forsake your old life, such as the world's take on sexual morality or its views on spiritual truth. If you fail to do this and continue to buy in to the world's philosophies, their influence will grow like yeast in a lump of dough (Galatians 5:8–9) until you eventually become confused again.

That is why the Bible commands, "Stand fast therefore in the liberty by which Christ has made us free, and do not be entangled again with a yoke of bondage" (Galatians 5:1 NKJV).

What's the Use?

*"The verdict has already been handed down—
'Guilty!'—so what's the use of protests or appeals?"*
JOB 9:28 MSG

Sometimes you may feel like Job: There is no use in complaining to God about your situation. He has already decided to punish you, and nothing you can say or do will change things. Usually this kind of hopelessness pervades your spirit when you have sinned and aren't sure if God has forgiven you.

Or it could come over you if God is convicting you about some fault or some wrong for which you have never apologized and you are unwilling to give up the habit or to make things right. Your own heart condemns you. After a while you may even forget why God is bearing down on you—and you just have a general feeling of hopelessness hanging like a cloud over your head.

Pray today and ask God to work in your heart and bring you to repentance. "If we confess our sins, He is faithful and just to forgive us our sins and to cleanse us from all unrighteousness" (1 John 1:9 NKJV). Then believe that He *has* forgiven you and move on.

Believing for the Impossible

"All this may seem impossible to you now. . . .
But is it impossible for me?"
ZECHARIAH 8:6 NLT

A handful of Jews had returned from captivity to Judah, but it was a long, hard journey, and few elderly people or children had come. But God promised that the streets of Jerusalem would be full of boys and girls at play and aged men and women sitting. This population explosion seemed impossible, but God said it would happen.

Sometimes God asks you, too, to believe the impossible. He realizes that to your limited knowledge the situation may seem hopeless, but He seeks to remind you that He is the all-powerful Creator of the heavens and the earth, and that nothing is impossible for Him.

Perhaps you have no problem with that but just don't believe that God cares enough about your circumstances to do the miracle. To this He says, "For I know the plans I have for you. . . plans to prosper you and not to harm you, plans to give you hope and a future" (Jeremiah 29:11 NIV).

With God on your side, your situation is far from hopeless.

Infertility

Desperate for Children

*When Rachel saw that she wasn't having
any children. . .she pleaded with Jacob,
"Give me children, or I'll die!"*
GENESIS 30:1 NLT

God put a natural desire in most women to have babies.
They may go for years enjoying the carefree single life,
with little desire to have children. Then the nesting
instinct kicks in with a vengeance and they simply *must*
have children to feel complete. God designed things
this way to ensure that the human race continues.

This is why Bible women who weren't able to bear
children went through such tremendous trials. We see
this with Sarah, and with Hannah and Elizabeth. But
no woman illustrates this better than Rachel. After she
had gone years without conceiving, she became so desperate that she literally felt like dying.

Many women today also struggle with infertility.
Although they have tried to get pregnant and have
undergone extensive fertility treatments, nothing
seems to work. And attempts at adoption face major
roadblocks.

But God has done miracles in the past, and He is
still able today. Don't give up hope. One way or another,
God can see to it that you have children.

Praying for a Son

If you'll. . .go into action for me by giving me a son,
I'll give him completely, unreservedly to you.
1 SAMUEL 1:11 MSG

Hannah was desperate for a son and promised the Lord that if He gave her a child, she would dedicate him completely to God. And look at the serendipitous way God worked! He desired to raise up a powerful prophet in Israel and did so through a humble woman's misery. When Hannah made a heartfelt surrender, dedicating her son utterly to God's purposes, God was able to act—and the great prophet Samuel was born!

You may not understand why God allows you to go through severe testings by keeping you from having children. But He may well have higher purposes in mind. Perhaps He prevents you from conceiving and giving birth because He wants you to adopt a wonderful child who desperately needs you to guide him or her into a high calling.

God often works in mysterious ways to bring about His will. He may lead you through the vale of tears, not because He doesn't love you, but because sometimes only such difficult paths bring about His will.

Content in God

Whom have I in heaven but You? And there is none
upon earth that I desire besides You.
PSALM 73:25 NKJV

It's a natural, good thing for a woman to desire to
become pregnant—even to long earnestly for a child
and to pray fervently for one. But there is a danger
even in desiring good things: If you become so obsessed
with something that you can't be happy without it, you
have exalted your desire above God.

In addition, God intends that you find your ultimate fulfillment in Him. You aren't born with this
desire. It has to be *learned*. Paul said, "I have learned
to be content whatever the circumstances" (Philippians
4:11 NIV).

Often Christians claim the promise: "Delight
yourself also in the LORD, and He shall give you the
desires of your heart" (Psalm 37:4 NKJV). They reason,
"I love God, so He is obligated to give me whatever
I want." But delighting yourself in the Lord means
choosing God's will, *whatever* it is, even if it runs contrary to your desires. And it sometimes does.

Certainly you should present your petitions to God.
But then rest them at His feet and submit to Him.

Injustice

Rescue the Oppressed

> *Be fair-minded and just. Do what is right!*
> *Help those who have been robbed;*
> *rescue them from their oppressors.*
> JEREMIAH 22:3 NLT

Some Christians refrain from getting involved with justice. They feel that believers should stick to spiritual matters. Paul wrote, "Let everyone be subject to the governing authorities, for there is no authority except that which God has established. . . . Whoever rebels against the authority is rebelling against what God has instituted" (Romans 13:1–2 NIV).

Many Christians take this to mean that they shouldn't even exercise their right to protest injustice. But this is taking Paul's meaning too far. Where would the fight to protect the unborn be if Christians hadn't protested abortion?

In fact, where would any number of issues be if Christians hadn't made their vote count during elections? One very effective way to address injustice is to vote for politicians who will make just laws. You can get involved and make a difference on the municipal level as well as the national level.

God is a God of justice, and He is intent on addressing injustice and oppression. So stand with Him today and do what is right.

A Recipe for Disaster

Whoever sows injustice reaps calamity.
PROVERBS 22:8 NIV

We become frustrated when criminals get away with evil by never being brought to account. This is bad enough when it involves individuals but is especially troubling when governments commit heinous acts against their own people.

You may opt not to watch the news, but turning a blind eye to the world's troubles is an avoidance technique, not a life skill. You don't need to follow the news obsessively, but it is not wise to ignore what is happening in your own country or your own city. How will you even know what to pray for? And you *should* pray.

You can also take comfort that the Bible speaks powerfully on this subject: "They that plow iniquity, and sow wickedness, reap the same" (Job 4:8 KJV). "Do not be deceived, God is not mocked; for whatever a man sows, that he will also reap" (Galatians 6:7 NKJV).

Don't fret if wicked oppressors seem to be having their way. "The wicked plots against the just" but "the Lord laughs at him, for He sees that his day is coming" (Psalm 37:12–13 NKJV).

Justice and Compassion

*"If I have despised the cause of my male or female
servant. . .what then shall I do when God rises up?"*
JOB 31:13–14 NKJV

God is a God of justice. Some people mistake justice
for vengeance and assume that God is harsh and vindictive. But this is wrong. God's acute sense of justice
stems from the fact that He is love (1 John 4:8) and
cares immensely for human beings. He desires to see
them receive what is fair. That is why He cautions
believers to treat others well. He wants you to be motivated by love, too.

You should fear God's power and justice. He will
reward you for the good you do but chastise you for the
wrong. Don't think that because you are the employer,
have the power to give orders and hire and fire, that
you can treat your employees however you wish. Even
man's society has laws giving workers rights—and God
does as well.

Christians are to love justice, and while Christian
bosses have a right to demand honest work for good
pay, they should be ruled by compassion. Be aware that
God is watching you (Colossians 4:1).

The Rights of the Poor

Woe unto them that decree unrighteous decrees. . .
to take away the right from the poor.
ISAIAH 10:1–2 KJV

God gave a number of laws in the Old Testament admonishing His people to care for the poor. In addition, their rights were enshrined in the legal code, and even kings were required to obey these laws.

Some rulers came up with new decrees to deprive the poor of their rights. For example, no one—not even the king—could force a poor man to sell his land if he didn't want to sell. But when King Ahab coveted the vineyard of a man named Naboth, the king's wife accused Naboth of blasphemy, then killed him and took his land. God judged these wicked rulers for their sin.

The principles of caring for the poor are still valid today. Even in the New Testament, when the apostles told Gentile churches the most important things they were to do, they commanded them to "remember the poor" (Galatians 2:10 NKJV).

Many modern Christians avoid helping the poor, thinking it is only an optional, peripheral suggestion. But it is actually an integral part of God's command to believers.

Insomnia

Sleep and Fear

When thou liest down, thou shalt not be afraid: yea,
thou shalt lie down, and thy sleep shall be sweet.
PROVERBS 3:24 KJV

Worry is one of the biggest hindrances to getting a good night's sleep—especially worry about finances. "The sleep of a laboring man is sweet. . .but the abundance of the rich will not permit him to sleep" (Ecclesiastes 5:12 NKJV). The rich toss and turn, worrying about losing their wealth. They know that all too often "riches. . .make themselves wings; they fly away" (Proverbs 23:5 NKJV).

Of course, many poor people lose sleep over money, too. They are not worried about dips in the stock market or a decline in the price of gold. Usually they worry about where they will get the money to pay their bills.

God's promise of sleep applies to everyone—rich and poor. The Scriptures promise, "You will keep him in perfect peace, whose mind is stayed on You" (Isaiah 26:3 NKJV). Stay focused on God's love for you and keep your mind filled with promises from His Word, and He will give you peace and rest. "God gives rest to his loved ones" (Psalm 127:2 NLT).

Sleeping in Peace

I will both lie down in peace, and sleep;
For You alone, O LORD, make me dwell in safety.
PSALM 4:8 NKJV

What's your sleep like when you are under pressure, facing stress, or being threatened? You probably have difficulty sleeping. You may hardly be able to rest at all.

When David's son Absalom led an army against him, David fled across the Jordan, where he gathered his own army. David penned a short psalm before the battle, declaring his trust in God. He proclaimed: "I lie down and sleep; I wake again, because the LORD sustains me. I will not fear though tens of thousands assail me on every side" (Psalm 3:5–6 NIV).

Think of the trouble David was in! But trusting that God shielded him and wouldn't allow him to be harmed, he lay down and slept peacefully, without tossing and turning all night. This took great faith. David had to look unswervingly at God or he would have worried himself sick.

You can't stop troubled thoughts from assailing your mind, but you can resolutely resist them. And as you do, God will give you peace, and you can sleep.

Unable to Sleep

You don't let me sleep. I am too distressed even to pray!
PSALM 77:4 NLT

Some people, when they wake up in the night and can't get back to sleep, spend time peacefully praying. As soon as they have communed with God for a while, they return to blissful sleep. This isn't the case with other people: They wake up but are too exhausted to properly focus. They *try* to pray but mostly just lie there longing for sleep.

When you are troubled, you are usually highly motivated to cry out to God. Asaph wrote, "When I was in distress, I sought the Lord; at night I stretched out untiring hands" (Psalm 77:2 NIV). Some nights, however, you may be *too* discouraged or troubled to pray. You may think that couldn't be, but it happens.

At times like that, instead of attempting to focus on a long prayer, shoot off short, sincere prayers every time you are able to focus, crying out for help. Quote faith-building verses. Sing hymns or songs of praise in your heart.

God will hear your prayers and answer, and after a while, the discouragement will dispel and sleep will return.

Job Loss

Enduring Prolonged Unemployment

*"Keep on asking, and you will receive what you ask for.
Keep on seeking, and you will find."*
MATTHEW 7:7 NLT

You may have been out of work so long that you have almost given up on finding employment. Or you may be working part-time for low wages. So you pray for God to change your situation. But when the drought continues, you may be tempted to give up.

In Elijah's day, Israel suffered from drought. After three and a half years, Elijah prayed for God to send rain. Then he told his servant to go look toward the sea. The servant returned, saying that he didn't see anything. Again Elijah prayed. Again he sent his servant. After doing this seven times, the servant finally saw a storm cloud.

Soon rain was falling heavily. The drought was over. But it didn't happen the first time Elijah prayed. He had to pray persistently before God answered (see 1 Kings 18:42–45). Jesus said that "men ought always to pray, and not to faint" (Luke 18:1 KJV).

So don't stop praying! You may have to wait awhile, but God will answer your prayers.

Getting Fired

"What's this I hear about you? You're fired.
And I want a complete audit of your books."
LUKE 16:2 MSG

Jesus told a parable about a wasteful overseer whose misdeeds finally caught up with him. As a result, his boss fired him. This man had it coming, but you may have lost your job through no fault of your own. But if your boss thinks that you were wasteful or negligent, you could receive the same treatment as this manager.

Perhaps you were unintentionally careless with important details. Perhaps there was a major miscommunication and you lost a large account. Whatever happened, you suddenly find yourself out of work, and you realize that your boss is not going to be a good reference on your future job application.

At times like this, you have to stay positive and trust that God will provide for you and take care of your reputation. Life isn't always fair, and you won't always be treated the way you deserve. But if you refuse to focus on the wrong, you will get back on your feet much quicker. So "let the peace of God rule in your hearts" (Colossians 3:15 NKJV).

Layoffs and Business Failures

"No craftsman of any craft shall be found in you anymore."
REVELATION 18:22 NKJV

You see it happening frequently these days: Giant store chains suffer prolonged losses, and to staunch the bleeding, they cut thousands of jobs or close stores in cities across the nation. And these are sometimes businesses offering vital services and products.

This is a foretaste of the total economic crash of the final days. When Babylon the Great, the worldwide commercial system, is destroyed, the Bible warns that "no craftsman of any craft shall be found in you anymore" (Revelation 18:22 NKJV). We see such breakdowns of basic services in war-torn nations and failed states today.

You may wonder how people survive such circumstances, but somehow they do—though to be sure, life is very difficult. But just such troubles have occurred many times before in earth's history, and God, knowing that they will happen again, promises to be with you.

He says, "Those who seek the LORD shall not lack any good thing" (Psalm 34:10 NKJV). It's important to trust God whether you are personally laid off or the world around you seems to be falling apart.

What Do I Do Now?

*"Now what? My boss has fired me. I don't have the
strength to dig ditches, and I'm too proud to beg."*
LUKE 16:3 NLT

Jesus told a parable about a rich man with vast wheat
fields and olive orchards. One day he discovered that
his manager was wasting his wealth. He fired him, of
course.

The manager knew word would quickly get out
and no one would hire him as a manager. But this was
the only skill he had. What could he do? Well, apparently
there was a major irrigation project in the area.
But ditch digging was backbreaking work and he was
no longer young. His only other option was to beg. But
that was too humiliating.

You may have lost a well-paying job due to a faltering
economy, but you otherwise identify with the
manager's question: "Now what?" You must either
become a minimum wage laborer or start panhandling.
Even if you do have skills to fall back on, you may see
a demotion in pay.

You will need courage and fortitude to make it
through this difficult time of transition. Don't give up
hope.

Job Stress

Work as unto the Lord

Work willingly at whatever you do, as though you were working for the Lord rather than for people.
COLOSSIANS 3:23 NLT

One of the most common sources of stress on the job is having a boss you don't like. Some bosses seem to have the idea that since they are boss, they can be blunt and inconsiderate, and their workers have to put up with them or be put out the door. Even bosses who are more considerate and reasonable still may do things that irk you.

The Bible has a solution: If you can't change your boss's attitude, change your own. Work as if you are working for Jesus, not for imperfect people. Peter advised, "Submit yourselves to your masters, not only to those who are good and considerate, but also to those who are harsh" (1 Peter 2:18 NIV). He was writing this to slaves, and some had truly harsh masters.

For the last two thousand years, this advice has helped countless believers put up with unpleasant work—and not only survive, but thrive.

If you simply can't stand your boss, the best option might be to look for a new job.

Intolerable Work Quotas

"Get your own straw wherever you can find it.
And not one brick less in your daily work quota!"
EXODUS 5:11 MSG

Some jobs have impossible work quotas. Workers may be expected to process a huge amount of units per day. In an effort to maximize profits and keep expenses down, many businesses try to squeeze as much work as possible out of their laborers for a minimum of pay.

They realize that quality is usually the first casualty of excessive work quotas, so they insist that you have to maintain quality no matter how much they pile on your plate. Either that or they give you the green light to produce substandard products.

Places of employment like that create constant stress, and while you can cope for a season, over time the situation will wear you down. You may have to stick with such a job for now to pay bills, but it is wise to keep your eyes open for alternate employment.

Pray that God gives you a better job with more reasonable expectations, and eventually the Lord will bring you out of "the house of bondage" (Exodus 13:14 NKJV).

A Heavy Workload

"We are unworthy servants
who have simply done our duty."
LUKE 17:10 NLT

You shouldn't expect lavish praise for doing what you are paid to do. And while a good boss will comment when you do your job competently, he or she is not obliged to do so. Praise is only due when you go beyond the call of duty.

Where work stress can come in is when your boss regularly requires you to do more than your job description. If you protest, you may be told that many people would be happy to have your job. And that may be true.

Now, you can carry the extra load for some time, but after a while the stress will get to you. Either that or you will need a fresh source of strength to buoy you up. That's where you must look to the Lord.

Jesus spoke to overworked laborers, saying, "Come unto me, all ye that labour and are heavy laden, and I will give you rest. Take my yoke upon you. . .and ye shall find rest unto your souls" (Matthew 11:28–29 KJV). Having spiritual peace can even help you carry a demanding workload.

Cheated Out of Wages

The wages you failed to pay the workers who mowed
your fields are crying out against you.
JAMES 5:4 NIV

Have you ever been cheated out of money? Perhaps
someone owed you for work you did but never paid
the final installment. Or they paid you nothing at all.
If you were depending on that income to pay bills, it
may have left you in a tight situation and very stressed.

Israel had many day laborers. They needed to be
paid at the end of each workday so that they could buy
food. So the Bible warned employers, "Each day you
shall give him his wages. . .for he is poor and has set his
heart on it; lest he cry out against you to the LORD, and
it be sin to you" (Deuteronomy 24:15 NKJV).

God warned, "If. . .they cry at all to Me, I will
surely hear their cry" (Exodus 22:23 NKJV). So rest
assured: Crooked employers won't forever get away
with nonpayment. God can to do what is needed to
get their attention. And if they don't respond in this
life, they will have to answer for their actions in the
next life.

Litigation

Settling Out of Court

"When you are on the way to court with your adversary, settle your differences quickly."
MATTHEW 5:25 NLT

Even if you do your job conscientiously and well, things can go wrong. You might have a misunderstanding with a client, or perhaps your client has unreasonable expectations. But the next thing you know, your client is taking you to court or threatening to do so.

This can be stressful, especially if the person suing you is aggressive and is attacking your reputation and integrity. You can lose sleep, get stomach cramps from worry, or experience anxiety. At times like this, you must look to the Lord and trust Him to defend you.

If you can, settling out of court is best. You can often do this if you refuse to get ruffled and maintain a polite, professional attitude. Sometimes you must go the extra mile to show goodwill and make your client happy.

However, if the other person is simply unreasonable, you need to stand firm and refuse to be intimidated. Read Ezra 4–6 to see how the Jewish people defended their rights using a legal document when they were being strongly opposed.

A Place for Lawsuits

If there is imposed on him a sum of money,
then he shall pay. . .whatever is imposed on him.
EXODUS 21:30 NKJV

Christians often seek to avoid litigation, even if they have a just cause, because of Paul's advice: "To have such lawsuits with one another is a defeat for you. Why not just accept the injustice and leave it at that?" (1 Corinthians 6:7 NLT).

But this refers to believers suing believers with unbelievers sitting in judgment, not to lawsuits in general. There are times to stand up for your legal rights and avoid someone gleefully cleaning you out. You have your family to provide for, after all. However, you should enter litigation prayerfully and judiciously.

And it works both ways. If someone does a careless job and you withhold payment until they finish it, they can take you to court—and things can get contentious. It's always best to try to reason with the other party and come to an agreement. There has to be some give-and-take.

As a believer, you are to be honest and just in your dealings. That doesn't include letting others rob you.

When Someone Sues You

*"If you are sued in court and your shirt is taken
from you, give your coat, too."*
MATTHEW 5:40 NLT

Jesus said that if someone sued you for the shirt off
your back, you were to let him have your coat as well.
In saying this, Jesus was acknowledging that sometimes believers would lose court cases, and He advised
giving more than the law required to show that you
are living undefeated and trusting God to care for you.

Some people protest that giving away so much
would leave you destitute, so Jesus couldn't have meant
to do this literally. But the point remains: The legal
system isn't necessarily the "justice system," so instead
of being defeated by injustices when they happen, you
must live victoriously.

Under Roman law, Christians had their entire
properties and possessions confiscated! The Bible says,
"When *all you owned* was taken from you, you accepted
it with joy. You knew there were better things waiting for you that will last forever" (Hebrews 10:34 NLT,
emphasis added).

Even if you lose in man's courts, be encouraged, for
"great is your reward in heaven" (Matthew 5:12 KJV).

Prodigal Children

When Children Go Astray

*I have no greater joy than to hear that
my children walk in truth.*
3 JOHN 1:4 NKJV

John wrote that his greatest joy was to know that his children were serving the Lord. And that is true of countless Christian parents today. Seeing your children grow up and claim their faith as their own is immensely rewarding.

On the other hand, many parents live in grief because their children have gone astray despite everything they were taught. When they entered their teen years, they stopped listening to counsel and ceased going to church. And once they became adults, they became fully set in their own ways. This is heartbreaking, even if they are not into a wild lifestyle. If they have simply drifted away and show no interest in spiritual things, parents may feel as if they have failed. But the fact is, God has no grandchildren. Every generation must decide for themselves to love and obey God—or not.

The good news is, if parents are faithful to pray for their wayward children, God may yet work in their hearts and bring those children back to Himself.

Praying for Prodigals

There is hope. . .saith the LORD, that thy children
shall come again to their own border.
JEREMIAH 31:17 KJV

When the Jews' enemies, the Babylonians, invaded Judah, they took thousands of Jews prisoner to Babylon. Those who had been taken captive wept bitterly. "By the rivers of Babylon we sat and wept" (Psalm 137:1 NIV). And the Jews who had been left in Judah, many of them elderly, grieved for their relatives and children.

Many parents can identify with these emotions. When their children get caught up in lifestyles of partying, alcohol, drugs, and sexual immorality, they, too, have gone to the land of the enemy. So parents pray "that they may come to their senses and escape the snare of the devil, having been taken captive by him" (2 Timothy 2:26 NKJV).

Even if you pray earnestly with tears, you may have to pray for years, but God hears you. He finally told the Jews of old, "Refrain thy voice from weeping, and thine eyes from tears: for. . .they shall come again from the land of the enemy" (Jeremiah 31:16 KJV). And you can have this same hope today.

Passive Rebellion

"Then the father told the other son, 'You go,' and he said,
'Yes, sir, I will.' But he didn't go."
MATTHEW 21:30 NLT

Usually when you think of a prodigal, you think of a
son or daughter living on his or her own and caught up
in a wild lifestyle. But a prodigal can simply be someone whose heart is far from God, even when still living
at home.

Jesus described two sons: When their father told
one son to go work in the vineyard, he openly refused.
The father then told his other son to go, and he replied,
"Yes, sir, I will." But he didn't. He had only said yes to
get his father off his back. Had he actually gone to the
vineyard, he would have done a lazy, careless job.

Many backslidden teens go to church and talk
the "God talk," but they are merely going through the
motions. They appear to be good Christians, but as one
writer confessed, "I was almost in all evil in the midst
of the congregation" (Proverbs 5:14 KJV). You need to
pray for such prodigals as much as for the openly rebel-
lious ones. God can change them, too.

Turning from Ruin

Repent, and turn yourselves from all your transgressions;
so iniquity shall not be your ruin.
EZEKIEL 18:30 KJV

It hurts you to see one of your children go astray and make the classical mistakes of youth. You are aware from your own experience and the experience of others of the price tag of a wild, disobedient lifestyle. It can utterly derail and ruin them.

You want to spare your children such a fate, so you warn them, you try to explain to them, but if they don't listen, all you can do is pray for them.

Let them know that although you disagree with their choices, you will always love them unconditionally, just like the father of the prodigal son (Luke 15:20–24). When they are ready to change, they will turn to the person who accepts them, not judges them.

Some people apparently need to hit rock bottom, to experience utter ruin, before they are willing to seek help. But pray that God will get you through to your children before that point. If they repent and turn from their willful ways, they can avoid the road to ruin. And many youth do.

Sickness

Staying Healthy

Some of you were sick because you'd lived a bad life,
your bodies feeling the effects of your sin.
PSALM 107:17 MSG

Some people believe that all illnesses are caused by
sin. If they suffer a stomach ailment, it is because they
failed to tithe. If they have arthritis, it is because they
spoke unkindly to someone. Certainly medical conditions can have spiritual and psychosomatic roots.
However, people bring most sickness on themselves
by their lifestyle choices. Those who overeat and don't
exercise are at a high risk of heart disease. People who
have a steady diet of junk food are prone to clogged
arteries and a plethora of other illnesses. And if they
abuse their bodies with alcohol or tobacco, they are in
danger of liver disease and cancer.

God has set up this physical world to operate
according to very practical rules. Violate those rules
and you will bring trouble on yourself. "You realize,
don't you, that you are the temple of God. . . ? No one
will get by with vandalizing God's temple, you can be
sure of that" (1 Corinthians 3:17 MSG). Take care of
your body. You will be glad you did.

God Restores Your Health

Whenever we're sick and in bed,
GOD becomes our nurse, nurses us back to health.
PSALM 41:3 MSG

God often heals His children, but we frequently take it for granted. Think of the powers of healing God has given your body. Time and again when you are sick or injured, your body is restored to health. Each time it happens, it is a miracle of His creative power. And many times when a sickness or injury is beyond your body's ability to heal, God supernaturally intervenes and reaches out to mend you.

Some Christians believe that the New Testament's emphasis on healing is a thing of the past, while others believe that Christians today can still lay claim to healing. God is still God, and He can and does heal.

"[God] forgives all your iniquities. . .heals all your diseases" (Psalm 103:3 NKJV). God still forgives all your sins, and there is no reason that He can't still heal. Of course, He doesn't act every time you want Him to. And He may allow you to be sick for quite some time. But you can be thankful for the times He does heal.

Protected from Illness

"You must serve only the Lord your God.
If you do. . .I will protect you from illness."
Exodus 23:25 NLT

God has made many promises in His Word to heal
sickness and to protect you from getting sick. This
verse explains one of the main conditions—you must
wholeheartedly serve God.

You may wonder, *Doesn't Mark 11:24 say that all I
need is faith? If I have enough faith I'll receive whatever
I ask for—including protection from illness.* Certainly
you do need faith, but there are conditions. The apostle
John wrote, "Whatsoever we ask, we receive of him,
because we keep his commandments, and do those
things that are pleasing in his sight" (1 John 3:22 KJV).

It's a lot better to be obedient and avoid getting
sick in the first place than it is to get sick and need
healing. And much of staying healthy comes from
obeying simple, commonsense rules, such as eating
healthily.

You may still get sick from time to time, even if
you are obedient, but God has promised, "Many are
the afflictions of the righteous, but the Lord delivers
him out of them all" (Psalm 34:19 NKJV).

Surgery

Trusting a Surgeon

"Healthy people don't need a doctor—sick people do."
LUKE 5:31 NLT

Many surgeries have become routine and are, statistically speaking, quite safe. Nevertheless, going under the knife can be a bit scary, especially for a major life-saving procedure. You need to know that the operation is absolutely required, and you need to trust that the surgeon is qualified to perform it.

Some people would rather God did an outright miracle, and if they have the kind of faith that actually receives miracles like that, good for them. But there is nothing wrong with availing yourself of the medical system. The Bible speaks positively of medicine, saying, "A merry heart does good like medicine" (Proverbs 17:22 NKJV).

Luke, who wrote nearly one-third of the New Testament, was a physician. He was a medical professional when Paul met him in AD 50, and he was still practicing medicine in AD 60 when Paul referred to him as "the beloved physician" (Colossians 4:14 NKJV).

You need to trust your surgeon. And you need to trust the Lord to give him even greater skill and make the operation a success.

The Mending Process

"For he wounds, but he also binds up;
he injures, but his hands also heal."
JOB 5:18 NIV

For a surgeon to remedy a serious condition, he has to first cut someone open. Then he can remove a tumor, fix a hernia, or repair a heart. Once he is done, he sews up the incision. He creates a wound, but only for the purpose of healing. It's a painful but necessary part of the healing process.

God often works the same way. Even though "he does not willingly bring affliction or grief to anyone" (Lamentations 3:33 NIV), He sometimes causes pain because, as He explains, "Those whom I love I rebuke and discipline" (Revelation 3:19 NIV).

God is the Great Physician, and He acts with great wisdom, skill, and love in everything He does. Even though it may sometimes look like He hasn't successfully resolved your problems, "we know that all things work together for good to those who love God" (Romans 8:28 NKJV). Even if you have postoperative pain, it is just part of the healing process.

Be thankful for lifesaving surgery, even if later it takes you a while to mend.

Toxic Friendships

Swayed by Peer Pressure

"You must not follow the crowd in doing wrong."
EXODUS 23:2 NLT

When you hear the words *peer pressure*, do you envision a teenager being urged by friends to commit an act of vandalism or to use drugs? The fact is, all ages are tempted to go along with a crowd. Think of coworkers trying to persuade you to help yourself to goods at your workplace or urging you to cheat on your taxes because "everyone does it."

God knows that the pressure to go along with the majority can be intense. You don't want to be a goody-goody. And you don't want to be persecuted by your workmates. Nevertheless, God commands you to buck the pressure and do what is right.

If you have been going along with the crowd and compromising your principles, you can stop doing it today. Approach the people pressuring you and tell them that your conscience won't allow you to continue. You have to do what's right. Pray for God to give you wisdom and a nonconfrontational approach. Then, if you have to lose their "friendship" over it, that is the way it has to be.

Nagging and Manipulating

She kept at it day after day,
nagging and tormenting him.
JUDGES 16:16 MSG

Some people are experts at getting what they want. What they lack in logical arguments or in persuasive ability, they make up for with sheer nagging skills. They know that if they continue whining, throwing tantrums, and insisting, you will often give in.

You may have a friend like that. She manipulates you by subjecting you to an emotional roller-coaster ride—at times threatening, then cajoling, then ranting, then laying guilt trips. If you are involved in such a friendship, it is wise to distance yourself from that person.

Sometimes, however, the nag is a family member whom you can't avoid. Solomon said, "A nagging spouse is like the drip, drip, drip of a leaky faucet; you can't turn it off, and you can't get away from it" (Proverbs 27:15 MSG).

So what do you do? You must learn to be firm with your decisions and remind the offender that he or she is nagging. This will, of course, upset the nag, but eventually she or he will give up. But you must stand your ground. After all, you can't always give in to nagging.

Unforgiveness

Reasons to Forgive

> *"If you do not forgive others their sins,*
> *your Father will not forgive your sins."*
> MATTHEW 6:15 NIV

When someone deliberately offends you, takes advantage of you, gossips about you, or harms you, God understands how hurt you feel. He also knows that it is a common reaction to want the other person to feel pain in return.

But only God can administer justice perfectly. So the Bible says, "Do not take revenge, my dear friends, but leave room for God's wrath, for it is written: 'It is mine to avenge; I will repay,' says the Lord" (Romans 12:19 NIV). Not taking matters into your own hands but instead trusting God to make things right takes faith.

God is well able to do that, but He needs you to unhook your fingers from the offense and give Him room to work. He even needs you to refrain from praying for vengeance and to forgive the offending party. After all, you have committed offenses yourself. "LORD, if you kept a record of our sins, who, O LORD, could ever survive?" (Psalm 130:3 NLT).

God forgives you. . .if you forgive others.

A Reason to Forgive

*Be ye kind one to another, tenderhearted,
forgiving one another, even as God for
Christ's sake hath forgiven you.*
EPHESIANS 4:32 KJV

God forgave all your sins, not because you deserved it—you didn't—but because of Christ's death on the cross.

For this reason, the Bible says that you also should forgive others who have hurt or offended you. Again, you don't do this because these people *deserve* to be forgiven—they probably don't—but because you are motivated by love. "For the love of Christ compels us" (2 Corinthians 5:14 NKJV). You are to forgive others the same way that God forgave you.

God is aware when others maliciously hurt you or use you, and He is not saying that what they do should simply be excused or overlooked because they are only human. But what He does ask you to do is to forgive—even though they are guilty.

You should especially be tenderhearted toward fellow Christians. You are to live in love, "forgiving one another, if anyone has a complaint against another; even as Christ forgave you, so you also must do" (Colossians 3:13 NKJV). If you do this, God will bless you richly.

Forgiveness Is Serious Business

*"This is how my heavenly Father will treat each
of you unless you forgive your brother
or sister from your heart."*
MATTHEW 18:35 NIV

God knows that if you have been deeply offended or
wounded, it takes time to process the pain, release it to
Him, and forgive the person who hurt you. But in the
end, you must forgive.

Jesus told a parable about a master who forgave his
servant an enormous debt. However, the servant then
seized a fellow servant who owed him a small sum and
threw him in jail. Angrily, the master asked, "Shouldn't
you have had mercy on your fellow servant just as I had
on you?" (Matthew 18:33 NIV). Then he ordered the
first servant to be afflicted in prison.

Jesus warned that God would treat believers the
same way if they didn't forgive others. You must forgive
others who have offended you, knowing that you yourself have been forgiven for many offenses.

God has had great mercy on you and continues to
shower you with compassion. If you are filled with His
love and walking in His Spirit, you will love those who
have offended you and show them mercy as well.

Why We Must Forgive

"Forgive us our debts,
as we also have forgiven our debtors."
MATTHEW 6:12 NIV

You may not feel a need to forgive others, but when you are in need of forgiveness, you are desperate for God to forgive. But there is a catch: In essence, Jesus said you should pray, "Forgive us our sins the exact same way we have forgiven those who have sinned against us."

But what if you have refused to forgive those indebted to you, who have sinned against you? The answer is clear: If you haven't forgiven others, then God is under no obligation to forgive you either. And He won't.

Some people think this is unfair. They think God should forgive them their many trespasses no matter how much bitterness and rage they have in their heart against His children. But should God forgive you if you have bitterness and anger against Him? No. "Whoever does not love their brother and sister, whom they have seen, cannot love God, whom they have not seen" (1 John 4:20 NIV). If you don't love others and forgive them, you don't love God, and God won't forgive you if you hate Him.

Violence

Avoiding Violence

*The answer's simple: Live right,
speak the truth. . .reject violence.*
ISAIAH 33:15–16 MSG

When someone cuts you off in traffic, nearly causing an accident, you are understandably angry. The same is true when someone physically attacks you, vandalizes your property, or lies about you. Anger has its rightful place, but the Bible warns, "Be angry, and do not sin" (Ephesians 4:26 NKJV). Many people sin when they are angry by committing violent acts against others.

Violence can quickly spiral out of control; you might hurt someone more than you intended to, and end up facing serious consequences. Plus, violence usually provokes more violence and vendettas; you create bitter enemies, and you, too, can end up hurt.

Psalm 7:16 (NIV) says, "The trouble they cause recoils on them; their violence comes down on their own heads." Violence is almost always a two-edged sword, hurting those who strike out as much as those they attack.

If you must take some form of action to protect yourself, be aware that there are a number of well-thought-out responses that avoid violence. Even when exercising your right to self-defense, use restraint.

Living by the Sword

"Put away your sword," Jesus told him.
"Those who use the sword will die by the sword."
MATTHEW 26:52 NLT

Many criminals live by the sword. They pack heavy firepower, sometimes even outgunning the police. They live and die in a violent world. But many people today engage in violence, even though they don't use guns. They give vent to their anger with their fists or whatever objects they can get ahold of.

If you find yourself expressing anger with violence, seek help to manage your temper. You may have avoided doing damage thus far, but it is only a matter of time before you do something that you will regret. You may traumatize loved ones, and though you apologize afterward, the damage will have been done.

Violence will also get you in trouble with the law. Eventually, if you fail to curb your temper, it will ensure that you suffer at the hands of another violent person. If you use the sword, you will die by the sword. It will take time, but it will certainly happen.

Trust God to work out situations, and turn away from violence. This will give God the needed space to work.

A Violent World

The earth also was corrupt before God,
and the earth was filled with violence.
GENESIS 6:11 NKJV

In Noah's day the earth was a very violent place, and Jesus tells us that "as the days of Noah were, so also will the coming of the Son of Man be" (Matthew 24:37 NKJV).

Every time you watch the news, you see incidents of violence. There is a steady stream of crime in the streets, in the malls, in the schools, and in the homes of our nation. You get the impression that the hour is late for planet earth.

But all this violence isn't just a statistic. Nor is it simply a fulfillment of Bible prophecy; real crimes are being committed against real people. You yourself or a member of your family may have been a victim of violent crime and know the trauma it brings. It can leave you shaken and insecure.

But know this also: "God has not given us a spirit of fear, but of power and of love," and "perfect love casts out fear" (2 Timothy 1:7; 1 John 4:18 NKJV). So let God fill you with His assurance and love.

Weakness

We Are Dust

He knows how weak we are;
he remembers we are only dust.
PSALM 103:14 NLT

God knows how prone to failure people are. He knows that you love Him and long to serve Him, but as Jesus observed, "The spirit is willing, but the flesh is weak" (Mark 14:38 NIV).

If you are strong-willed, you may be frustrated by how weak others seem, by how easily they succumb to temptation or disappoint you. You may be disappointed at how spiritually immature someone is and feel like blurting out in exasperation, "Come on! You can do better than that! Pull yourself up by your bootstraps!"

Although God Himself wishes that such people would mature faster, don't forget that He constantly has mercy on them. Just before saying that He knows how weak people are, mere dust, the Bible says, "The LORD is like a father to his children, tender and compassionate to those who fear him" (Psalm 103:13 NLT). This isn't to excuse people who are flagrantly sinning, but it is a reminder to have compassion on those who are weak in areas where you are strong.

We Are But a Shadow

We are but of yesterday, and know nothing,
because our days upon earth are a shadow.
JOB 8:9 KJV

Compared to God, people have the lifespan of a moth. Even compared to the angels, we are just flickering shadows fleeting across the ground. We are a thin mist, quickly vanishing in the morning light.

As David prayed, "You have made my days as handbreadths, and my age is as nothing before You; certainly every man at his best state is but vapor" (Psalm 39:5 NKJV). A "handbreadth" is one of the smallest biblical measurements, only the width of a palm.

Human beings live about seventy to eighty years, which may seem like a long time, but to God it is as if we were born yesterday. Many people are just beginning to acquire wisdom and accomplish their life's objectives at that age—when their strength fails and life ends.

In the beginning, God didn't make humans so futile and weak. God designed us to be immortal. We are literally a shadow of what we were intended to be. It's good to keep this in mind when you are tempted to get proud about your beauty, your strength, or your accomplishments.

When You Are without Might

He giveth power to the faint; and to them that
have no might he increaseth strength.
ISAIAH 40:29 KJV

When you feel weak and unable to cope, and life has completely knocked the wind out of you, you may think it is all over. But God can breathe new strength into you. The Bible is clear: Precisely when you are at the point that you are ready to collapse physically or are fainthearted and lacking the will to continue, God can help you.

God comes to those in truly desperate straits. When you have absolutely no might left at all, and are at the point of buckling, that is when the Lord shows up and supplies you with power. "You shall receive power when the Holy Spirit has come upon you" (Acts 1:8 NKJV).

The Lord increases your strength to where you are able to face your day, able to confront your problems and gain the victory over them. But you have to believe that God is both willing and able to do that for you, and then receive His strength.

"Be strong in the Lord and in the power of His might" (Ephesians 6:10 NKJV).

When You Are Weak

And he said unto me, My grace is sufficient for thee:
for my strength is made perfect in weakness.
2 CORINTHIANS 12:9 KJV

Perhaps you have enjoyed good health most of your life and have been able to enjoy your work, provide for yourself, and do pretty much whatever you needed to. But what happens if you begin to suffer from poor health or disability, or experience the limitations of old age, and find yourself unable to do many of the things you did before?

Suddenly you are not as independent as you used to be. You find that you have neither the strength nor the energy to do many day-to-day tasks. Having limitations on your ability to care and provide for yourself can be immensely frustrating.

One thing you find out quickly is that you pray more and have to depend on God to take care of you and to make things happen. And you learn to depend on the kindness of family and friends (1 Timothy 5:4–5). This can be a very humbling experience, but at the same time, it can be a very spiritually enriching period of life.

Ministering Though Weak

I was with you in weakness,
in fear, and in much trembling.
1 CORINTHIANS 2:3 NKJV

When Paul preached the gospel in Corinth, he had a very effective ministry. You may think, *Of course! He was the apostle Paul, after all.* But Paul was a man, subject to the same limitations and fears as you. He later confessed, "I was with you in weakness, in fear, and in much trembling."

Because Paul knew that he wasn't capable, but had to depend on the Lord, God was able to work mightily through him. Then Paul knew that God had done the work. This is often the way it is: God asks you to step out and attempt great things no matter how weak you feel. To think that you are in over your head, that there is no bottom beneath your feet, may be scary, but God is there.

He says, "Do not fear, for I am with you. . . . I will strengthen you and help you; I will uphold you with my righteous right hand" (Isaiah 41:10 NIV). If you know that God is there to catch you, you can attempt great things.

Worry

Give God Your Worries

Give all your worries and cares to God,
for he cares about you.
1 PETER 5:7 NLT

Everyone worries from time to time, but some people are especially prone to it. Whichever category you fall into—but especially if you are a constant worrier—God's solution is to give Him all your cares. Why? Because a constant state of anxiety isn't good for your mental or physical health. Psalm 37:8 (NKJV) says, "Do not fret—it only causes harm."

There are two more reasons why you should hand all your worries and cares to God. The first is that He genuinely cares about you and doesn't want you to suffer needlessly. Knowing the human tendency to want to try to sort everything out, He made it a command: "Give all your worries and cares to God."

The second reason is that God is all-powerful and is, in fact, the only one in existence capable of resolving all your problems.

"Let us therefore come boldly unto the throne of grace," lay the problem at His feet, and trust Him to "help in time of need" (Hebrews 4:16 KJV).

Worrying Is Useless

> *"Can any one of you by worrying*
> *add a single hour to your life?"*
> MATTHEW 6:27 NIV

Not only can you not add one hour to your life by worrying, but worry will probably cut years from your life. Anxiety, prolonged over time, has a negative effect on your health, leading to insomnia, stomach disorders, and—in worst-case scenarios—heart attacks.

Jesus warned that stress would be a major killer in the last days, with "men's hearts failing them from fear" (Luke 21:26 NKJV). So worrying is not only useless, it is worse than useless and highly detrimental.

So many people worry about trivial things. Yet Jesus admonished you not even to worry about vitally important things. He said, "Therefore do not worry, saying, 'What shall we eat?' or 'What shall we drink?' or 'What shall we wear?'" (Matthew 6:31 NKJV).

Certainly God expects you to work to provide the money you need to live, so He is not advising you to be lazy or complacent. But He commands you not to worry. Even if your financial situation is unstable, you do well to remember that God is your ultimate provider.

One Day at a Time

*"Do not worry about tomorrow, for tomorrow
will worry about itself. Each day has
enough trouble of its own."*
MATTHEW 6:34 NIV

Jesus warned against the futility of worrying about the future, focusing on trouble that hasn't even happened yet. Doing so distracts you from important things you should concentrate on today.

Certainly if there are large events or problems looming on the horizon—for example, if you are responsible to organize a banquet—you can't ignore giving thought to them. But you are simply to make whatever plans you can then commit the unresolved details to God in prayer, not worry about them.

The difference between *planning for* tomorrow and *worrying about* tomorrow is that worrying often involves getting your eyes on the entire problem at once, then despairing that you can't handle it; whereas planning means having the faith that you can meet the challenge if you pray and take practical steps to meet it.

When Jesus said that today already has enough troubles that require your attention, He was basically advising you to keep your eyes on God, moment by moment, not on your problems.

Worry Weighs You Down

Worry weighs us down; a cheerful word picks us up.
PROVERBS 12:25 MSG

If you are concerned about your finances, your health, a wayward child, a relationship, or any number of other things, you will be tempted to worry. This is especially true if the situation looks difficult and things stand a very real chance of not working out in your favor.

At times like that, a cheerful word can encourage you. It doesn't even have to be the total solution to your problems, such as, "The check just arrived!" or "The test came back negative!" It can simply be a cheerful word, someone letting you know that he or she cares— because that lets you know that *God* cares.

The reason this can be so encouraging is that although you would like God to resolve things at once, your immediate need is to know that God sees your situation, cares, and will be coming through for you. This is why David prayed, "Send me a sign of your favor. . . . For you, O LORD, help and comfort me" (Psalm 86:17 NLT).

This is also a good reason to be sure to comfort and encourage others.

Also from Barbour Books

Here is a practical guide of short prayer starters that will help readers pray confidently during difficult times. From illness and death to divorce and job loss, dozens of topics are covered. Each section opens with a short devotional thought and applicable scripture. Great as a ministry resource or for a personal library, *Prayers for Difficult Times* is a must-have tool for anyone searching for a stronger prayer life.

DiCarta / 978-1-63058-661-4 / $12.99